WHAT MY LIFE TAUGHT ME ABOUT TEACHING

Identity, Music, and Becoming an Educator

Richard A. Fields, Ed.D.

Independently Published

FOREWORD

I first met Richard in New York at SUNY Purchase College by chance, in the music building where he was a student. He told me he was studying trumpet performance there, and my heart skipped a beat. Though I did not play the trumpet myself, my middle school son had just been assigned the instrument by his teacher, much to his chagrin. I knew that learning the trumpet was going to be a much bigger challenge for his ADHD mind to persevere with than the drums he had requested, so I sought some advice from the future Dr. Fields. It did not take long for my son to respond to the effective encouragement and instruction that Richard patiently gave him. Soon he was producing notes that got him small solos in his middle school band, which eventually turned into lead trumpet throughout his high school years.

Richard is an amazing performer, compassionate teacher, and a much admired human being. I have known him and have worked side by side with him in our church community for over two decades now, and I am very grateful to be a close friend of his.

Teaching for Richard is not a job; it is a calling—and one he takes very seriously. He brings out the best in people he instructs and inspires vision even in those he has just met.

Much of this has been formed from the incredible challenges he has lived through in his life by facing each of them head on. He knows what works: a stubborn refusal to give in. His intransigence to persevere has produced this "brave as a lion; empathetic as a best friend" mentor and teacher that is certainly leaving its mark.

I am thrilled he has written this book. It is a page turner. Though he will want you to "slow down" and ruminate, your heart will crave the next chapter. It will bring you laughs and tears, but most importantly, you will be challenged in the way you frame your thinking about how to effectively teach others.

We need this book today. Those who thrive in this sped-up world are constantly evaluating, changing, and adjusting—questioning what is effective, what is limited.

This book's relevance and authenticity are undeniable, making a world of difference to those who dare put it into practice. It is an upward call to being vulnerable and fully human as an inspiration to those you influence through your teaching. All of us have had our battles, victories, and defeats, and each of these has helped mold us into the unique individual we are. We all have a story to tell, to live out, to translate into others, to inspire those around us.

So, plunge in! Take those heroic, brave steps. Redefine your personal teaching.

As Richard so beautifully illustrates: *Teaching is a relational craft.*

You have more power than you realize.

—*Jim Brown*

PREFACE

Why This Book Exists

This book was not written to offer answers.
It was written to tell the truth.

For a long time, I wrestled with whether I should write it at all—not because I lacked stories or convictions, but because I did not want this work to feel performative, prescriptive, or shaped for approval. If I was going to put something into the world, it needed to come from an honest place. It needed to reflect lived experience without shortcuts, mythology, or pretending the journey was cleaner than it actually was.

What follows is not a success story in the traditional sense.
It is a story of becoming.

Becoming a musician.
Becoming an educator.
Becoming a person shaped by movement, instability, faith, failure, persistence, and care.

These identities did not develop separately. They collided, overlapped, contradicted one another, and—over time—began to inform each other. This book traces that arc: not only the visible milestones, but the quieter moments where identity was tested, redefined, and rebuilt.

In many ways, this work grows out of my doctoral research, which focused on identity, access, and persistence among musicians and educators from historically underrepresented backgrounds. What I encountered there—and later recognized in myself—was a shared tension: the struggle to locate personhood within institutions that often prioritize performance, productivity, or conformity over humanity.

This book continues that inquiry, but inward.

It asks what it means to pursue excellence while navigating systems not designed with you in mind. What it costs to persist. What happens when an identity you worked tirelessly to build begins to fracture—and what it takes to assemble something more sustainable in its place.

This is not a manifesto.
It is not a method.
And it is not a blueprint.

It is a reflection on formation—on how a life, fully lived, shapes how we teach, how we lead, how we listen, and how we care. On how identity is not discovered all at once, but assembled slowly through choice, constraint, and courage.

If you are an educator, an artist, a student, or someone still finding language for who you are and who you are becoming, I hope you see something of yourself in these pages—not because our paths are the same, but because the questions are often shared.

This book exists to say:

You are not alone in the struggle to belong.
Your story is still unfolding.
And the work of becoming—while difficult—is deeply human.

Who This Book Is For

This book is written for educators, artists, musicians, and leaders who want to understand the human journey behind professional roles.

It is for aspiring teachers wondering what the work might ask of them beyond lesson plans and credentials. For practicing educators carrying more than they anticipated, learning—sometimes painfully—that teaching is as much about identity and endurance as it is about content. For artists navigating the tension between passion and sustainability, excellence and access. And for leaders who want to better understand the unseen conditions that shape how people show up in institutions.

It is also for those whose lives have shaped their work—often without consent—and who are still making sense of how hardship, movement, faith, loss, or failure quietly forged their capacity to lead, teach, or create.

This book does not promise easy answers.
What it offers instead is companionship.

A reminder that becoming is rarely linear, rarely clean, and rarely solitary—and that the work we are called to do is often shaped long before we consciously choose it.

An Invitation

You do not need to agree with everything in this book.
You do not need to share my experiences, beliefs, or conclusions.

This is not a prescription.
It is an invitation.

An invitation to notice how your own life has shaped the way you teach, lead, create, or serve. To sit with moments that may feel affirming—and others that may feel uncomfortable. To ask better questions about who you already are, and how you arrived there.

If this book does its work, it will not tell you who to become. It will simply create space for you to listen more carefully to what your life has already been teaching you.

Contents

1 The Beginning: Growing Up Between Worlds

Core Question

*What did constant movement teach me about belonging and identity—
before I had language for either?*

I remember always doing something a little wild, even as a
child.

One moment stands out with particular clarity. I decided—
quite confidently—that it would be a good idea to pretend I
was Superman and jump from our second-story bedroom
window. I don't remember hesitation. I remember certainty. I
remember believing I could fly.

I also remember thinking it was hilarious afterward—
especially when my sister later watched me walk calmly
through the front door as if nothing had happened.

I was lucky I didn't break my legs.

That moment has stayed with me not because it was reckless,
but because it revealed something essential about how I have
always moved through life. I have often leapt—into new
environments, unfamiliar identities, and uncertain futures—
before fully understanding the consequences. Sometimes that
instinct carried me forward. Sometimes it humbled me.
Always, it taught me.

Long before I had language for identity, belonging, or
resilience, I was already learning them through movement.

Miami (Ages 0–5): Attachment and Safety

I was born on December 12, 1983, at Jackson Memorial Hospital in Miami, Florida. From my earliest memories, I was deeply attached to my mother—fully engaged, fully present, unmistakably a mama's boy. In public, my small hand was always reaching for hers. I needed to know she was close.

There's a moment from around age four that still lives vividly in my memory.

I grabbed the wrong mama.

It didn't last long. Someone noticed, laughter followed, and I was quickly reunited with my own mother. But the memory stayed—not because it was funny, but because it captures something essential about who I was in those early years: a child rooted in attachment, closeness, and connection.

That bond mattered. It shaped how I related to people, how I searched for safety, and how I understood belonging long before I had the language to name any of it.

Movement (Ages 5–11): A Life in Motion

This is not a linear story.

My early childhood did not move neatly from year to year, and our relocations did not align cleanly with school calendars. It helps to name the geography first—and then return to the moments within each place that mattered most.

- From birth through age five, I lived in Miami.
- At five, we moved to Charleston, South Carolina.
- At six and seven, we returned to Miami.

- At eight and nine, we lived in Philadelphia.
- At ten, it was Miami again.
- At eleven, Jamaica—followed by yet another return to Miami.

This is not a timeline to memorize.
It is context.

What follows are narrative snapshots—moments that shaped my character, seeded my academic identity, and revealed early patterns of resilience and perseverance.

Charleston, South Carolina (Age 5): Innocence Before Awareness

When we first moved to Charleston, it felt exciting. I remember it as an adventure rather than a rupture. We traveled frequently between Miami and Charleston for my parents' business, and those trips felt grounding—movement without fear, change without loss.

At that age, relocation felt like possibility.

Kindergarten itself was not particularly challenging. What I remember most is eating glue, watching *The Little Mermaid*, taking naps, and waiting for the day to end. I don't recall learning much academically, but I do remember having fun. My teachers were kind. School felt safe, light, uncomplicated.

Looking back, what stands out most is not what I learned—but what I had not yet been asked to confront. I had not been required to explain myself, adapt quickly, or navigate difference.

Then something shifted.

We were staying in a hotel room when the police arrived. I remember adult voices, confusion, and fear—standing outside in the cold while officers questioned my parents. I didn't understand what was happening. I only knew something serious was unfolding.

The officers were kind to us as children. What unsettled me was not their presence, but the sudden change in atmosphere—the realization that the world could turn tense without warning.

Around that same time, I remember quiet exchanges, sudden silences, and an unspoken expectation that I keep moving and not ask questions. I couldn't name what I was witnessing. I only felt its weight.

This was my first encounter with the idea that adult worlds carry realities children are often asked to absorb without explanation.

Miami (Ages 6–7): Learning Under Instability

After Charleston, we returned to Miami. I was about six years old and entering first grade—an important turning point in my academic life.

Coming out of a kindergarten experience with little rigor, I was suddenly placed into a learning environment that felt intense. I was completely unprepared. Early in the year, I took a placement assessment and understood none of it. The page might as well have been written in hieroglyphics.

Panicked and confused, I tried to copy answers from a classmate. When the teacher caught me, I was sharply rebuked. What stayed with me was not the discipline itself, but the shame. I didn't yet know how to ask for help.

After that moment, I made a quiet promise to myself: I would never cheat on a test again.

And I didn't.

Once the material was actually taught, something shifted. A pattern emerged that would repeat throughout my schooling: I often started the year as an average student—but by the end, I became one of the strongest in the class.

By the end of first grade, my teacher asked me to lead the class in singing "Kumbaya." I resisted until she insisted. Reluctantly, I did it.

First grade ended in success—not because it was easy, but because I learned how to learn.

Second grade was different.

I carried a quiet belief that my teacher did not like me. I was frequently corrected, often scolded, and over time I began to assume something was wrong with me.

At seven years old, my conclusion was simple:

I hated second grade.

That impression lingered. I walked away believing that some teachers decide who you are before you ever have the chance to show them.

Philadelphia (Ages 8–9): Separation and Survival

My mother made the decision to move our family from Miami to Philadelphia. She believed it was the safest option available at the time. She had family there, which meant we had a place to land while she worked to determine what came next.

In Philadelphia, we experienced instability. There were periods when we stayed in shelters. At the time, it didn't feel frightening or shameful. I met new kids, made friends, and even had moments of fun. Only later did I understand how exhausting that season must have been for my mother.

Eventually, we moved into a government-assisted apartment. I remember it as a good home—safe and grounding, even if temporary. We also received food assistance. I didn't associate that with poverty. What I understood was simple: we were never hungry, and we always had a place to sleep.

Then my mother received a job opportunity that required her to return to Miami—without us.

For the first time in my life, I was separated from her.

Entering third grade, I remember being angry—getting into fights, especially if anyone said anything about my mother. Academically, I neither excelled nor declined. My energy went into managing grief.

What stands out most from that year is my third-grade teacher. She noticed what I was carrying and responded with care rather than punishment. She allowed a friend and me to spend time with her during the day—playing games, simply being present.

It was the first time I saw an educator lead with empathy rather than authority.

Fourth grade brought the same ache. When my mother visited, my entire life lit up.

One day, after a test, the teacher paused at my paper.

"Richard," she said, "you got the highest score in the class. A perfect score."

For the first time, I wondered if maybe I wasn't so bad at this school thing after all.

Soon after, we returned to Miami.

Character Tested: Stealing (Age 10)

Back in Miami with my mother, I was a happy and well-adjusted ten-year-old. Family meant security.

But there were moments that quietly tested my character.

It began with small acts—candy items here and there. I knew it was wrong, but my internal compass was still forming. By fifth grade, influenced by a friend, the behavior escalated.

One day, a man in plain clothes stopped us. He had been watching the entire time. He took us into a back room and told us we were going to jail.

I was terrified.

When my mother came to pick me up, shame flooded me—not just fear of consequences, but the pain of having disappointed her.

That moment ended that chapter of my life.

I vowed never to steal again.

And I didn't.

Not because of fear alone, but because I never forgot how quickly something thrilling revealed itself to be deeply misaligned with the person I wanted to become.

Reflection: What Movement Taught Me

Looking back, I see clearly how much educators mattered in my life—especially those who led with empathy. They cared when care was not required. They noticed when it would have been easier not to.

Movement itself was not the true disruptor. Much depended on temperament—and on the care children received while navigating change.

For me, movement was difficult, but formative.

It shaped my resilience, awareness, and becoming.

Practice for Educators (Chapter 1)

Before we evaluate behavior, achievement, or effort, we must ask a harder question:

What might this student be carrying into the room today?

Movement, instability, and transition do not affect all children the same way. Often, the difference is not temperament alone—but the presence of adults willing to notice.

Before we ask students to perform, comply, or succeed, we might first ask:

Have I helped them feel safe enough to try?

Because sometimes, the most powerful lesson we offer has nothing to do with content.

It is the quiet assurance that:

You are seen.
You belong here.
You do not have to carry everything alone.

2 Becoming Something I Never Planned to Be

Guiding Question

What happens when persistence—rather than intention—begins to shape identity?

Character Tested: Choice Without Applause

This period of my life was deeply confusing. Family circumstances were unstable. School felt uneven. And like most ten-year-olds, I was simply trying to find my footing. I was learning—slowly—how to navigate friendships, influence, and my own emerging sense of self.

Around that time, I spent a lot of time with two brothers who lived nearby. They had a reputation for getting into trouble, but I never used that as a measure of whether they deserved friendship. With me, they were kind and easy to be around. We played video games, talked sports, and passed time the way kids do. I never had issues with them.

There was one moment, though, that stands out.

One afternoon, they offered me cigarettes. I tried one—just once.

Almost immediately, I knew it wasn't for me. Not because someone had warned me, but because something felt off. For years, I had encouraged family members to quit smoking, knowing it wasn't healthy. The contradiction hit me hard. I didn't want to be the kind of person who spoke one way and lived another. That single experience was enough.

I was done.

Not long after, they offered me marijuana.

That, too, was an easy no.

There was no speech. No fear. No pressure. I simply wasn't interested. Whatever I was becoming, I knew it didn't include that path. Our friendship continued—but only within boundaries that felt right to me: sports, video games, snacks. Like many childhood friendships, it eventually faded.

Years later, I learned that both brothers struggled deeply with school and authority. I don't believe either of them finished high school. They weren't bad kids. They were kids without direction, without consistent guidance, without the right support at the right moment.

I think about them often.

That experience taught me something important—not about cigarettes or drugs, but about decision-making. No one congratulated me for saying no. No adult intervened. Life simply moved on.

And yet, it was one of the first times I realized that character is often formed quietly—in moments that pass without recognition or applause.

Miami, Florida (Age 11): Shifting Ground

At the start of sixth grade, I was still in Miami, attending the middle school I had been assigned to. Academically, I was doing fine—not exceptional, not struggling—somewhere in the middle. Then I learned that my mother had accepted another job opportunity.

The position required her to live with her client as a full-time home health aide. In many ways, the job fit her nature perfectly. She was a magnificent caretaker—thoughtful, detail-oriented, deeply service-minded. That was simply who she was, and it was why she was so good at her work.

Her new role meant that I would move in with my father.

Until then, my dad had never been my primary caretaker. In some ways, it felt novel—almost exciting. He was a Vietnam veteran and lived with a number of health challenges. Much of his life revolved around the VA hospital in Miami, medications, and long stretches of watching television. I remember noticing how many pills he took each day and thinking, in my child's way, *As long as he's okay, I guess this is okay.*

He lived in VA-supported housing, a place largely occupied by elderly residents. I was quiet and kept to myself, but my presence there was still an issue. It didn't take long before it became clear that this arrangement wasn't going to last.

That was when my parents made the decision to send me to Jamaica.

Jamaica (Age 11): Displacement, Perspective, and the First Spark

I arrived in Jamaica indifferent—and then immediately overwhelmed.

The culture shock was intense. I had gone from a low-income life in the United States to what would be considered a middle-class life on the island. At the time, my thinking was simple and unfiltered: I'd rather be poor in the U.S. than middle class in a third-world country.

Nothing felt familiar. I had to boil water for baths because I wasn't used to cold showers. The bugs devoured me so badly that a single bite required medication. There were only two television channels, both playing the same programs every day. I was bored beyond belief.

To make matters worse, my mother was back in the States.

I was miserable.

I watched the same five movies over and over—*Beauty and the Beast* included—until I could recite them by heart. I longed for video games, cable television, and the everyday comforts I had taken for granted as an American kid.

And yet, Jamaica changed me.

For the first time, I encountered extreme poverty up close. A young boy who lived down the street wore the same blue pair of underwear every day. He had nothing else. That image lodged itself deep inside me. I remember seriously considering giving him my clothes—I had so much, and he had so little—but I didn't know how to do it.

I was also introduced to farm life: cows, goats, chickens—the realities behind food. When someone casually told me that an animal I had asked about was what we ate for dinner the night before, it unsettled me. I was once asked to help slaughter a chicken, and I couldn't do it. I simply didn't have it in me.

School in Jamaica was different as well. I attended a modest private school. Academically, I wasn't challenged; the standards felt low compared to what I had known. The one upside was that I advanced a grade. Even then, it felt easy.

Music entered my life quietly there. We played the recorder a few times in school—nothing remarkable on its own. But next door lived a group of older boys, and one of them played the drums. Watching him, something clicked.

Whoa. Teach me how to do that.

I had always been drawn to instruments. Whenever I saw a piano, I lingered longer than most. I loved music—especially rap. Tupac was my soundtrack. But Jamaica was the first time I saw someone my age be an instrumentalist.

That mattered.

I lived in Jamaica for about eight months. I learned a great deal, lost weight from constant movement and better food, and experienced one of the most formative transitions of my early life.

I didn't know it then, but something essential had shifted.

Back to Miami: Familiar Ground, New Stakes

My family was eventually able to bring me back to Miami, and I once again lived with my dad—this time in a small studio apartment within an older-adults housing community. I cannot overstate how happy I was to be back in the United States—back to hot water, cable television, air conditioning, and the everyday comforts I had missed.

Most of all, I was home.

I returned to my previous middle school and was placed back into my proper grade: seventh. At the time, it felt like a setback. In hindsight, it was the beginning of a turning point.

During this period, I was exposed—almost accidentally—to formal instrumental music instruction.

That exposure would quietly alter the trajectory of my life.

The Schedule That Changed Everything

At the start of seventh grade, I received my class schedule and immediately noticed something that felt wrong.

Band.

There had to be a mistake.

Up to that point, my identity had been firmly rooted in sports. I was good at basketball, football, and baseball. I had coordination, speed, and confidence. I believed—quite sincerely—that I was destined for the NFL. Sports made sense. Physical education made sense.

Band did not.

I marched into my guidance counselor's office and said, "Please take me out of band. You've made a terrible mistake. I belong in P.E."

She calmly encouraged me to try it.

Angrily and reluctantly, I agreed.

The $35 Problem

In the first few weeks during band class, we were introduced to different instruments and told there would be a materials fee. I immediately knew my family could not afford it. In my mind, this was my way out.

Freedom.

Somehow, my father came up with thirty-five dollars for a trumpet mouthpiece. I was shocked—and disappointed. That money mattered. It meant I was officially stuck in band.

I chose the trumpet for one simple reason: it only had three buttons. Compared to the other instruments, it looked manageable.

Nearly thirty years later, I know how wrong that assumption was.

Seventh-grade band itself was unremarkable. We played simple songs—"London Bridge," "Mary Had a Little Lamb." I didn't enjoy it. By the end of the year, I was convinced I would never touch the trumpet again.

Advanced Band (Against My Will)

Eighth grade began, and to my horror, I was placed into advanced band.

This felt like an even bigger mistake than the year before. I returned to the guidance counselor and protested again. Surely this time, there had been an error.

Before school started, I placed my trumpet mouthpiece in a kitchen drawer. I nearly threw it away. The only reason I didn't was simple: we were poor, and that mouthpiece had cost thirty-five dollars.

No dreams.
No intention.
Just practicality.

When I was told to "get your mouthpiece out of the kitchen drawer and get on with it," I did.

The Embarrassment—and the Decision

I dreaded the trumpet. And judging by the sounds coming out of it, the trumpet dreaded me too.

I was easily one of the worst trumpet players in the school. Every time I was asked to play, I felt exposed—embarrassed in a way I wasn't used to.

In most areas of my life, I was never the worst. This was new.

So I made a quiet decision:

I didn't need to be the best.
I just refused to be the worst.

I took one of the school's old, battered trumpets home and started trying to figure it out.

Practice in a One-Room Apartment

My father and I lived in a one-room studio in downtown Miami. There was no place to practice. I played either outside or in the bathroom.

Our band standard was the B-flat concert scale. I practiced it relentlessly—whole notes, half notes, quarter notes, eighth notes—over and over again.

Sometimes my dad would yell, "Boy! Stop making all that noise."

I practiced like that for about two months.

No one at school knew.

The Walk to Second Chair

Then came chair placement auditions.

I hated them. I always made mistakes. My friends laughed. It was gut-wrenching.

This time was different.

When my turn came, I played my scale—nearly perfectly.

My band director held up two fingers.

I stood up and walked to second chair.

That walk was terrifying.
It was validating.
It was quiet.
And it changed everything.

When Music Became Part of Me

From that moment on, music took hold.

At thirteen, I went to the Miami-Dade Public Library and checked out every book I could find on trumpet and brass playing. I left with nearly ten books and a stack of recordings.

One recording stayed with me: the Chicago Brass Quintet. I listened constantly, wondering how human beings could make instruments sound like that.

By the end of eighth grade, I was second chair in my middle school band—and sixth chair across all of Miami-Dade County.

It had taken about eight months.

I didn't fully understand what I had done.

I was just along for the ride.

Faith, Music, and Staying

There was one more defining development during this time: faith.

I won't overstate it—but I won't omit it either.

Alongside music, faith became an anchor. Quiet. Grounding. Consistent.

Together, they carried me forward.

Reflection: The Power of Staying

Looking back, this chapter taught me something essential:

Identity does not always begin with intention.
Sometimes, it begins with staying.

Staying when you're embarrassed.
Staying when you're uncomfortable.
Staying when you want to quit.

No one told me I was talented. No one predicted a future in music. What changed everything was persistence, access, and one adult who allowed the process to unfold.

That combination would later define not only my relationship with music—but my understanding of education itself.

Practice for Educators (Chapter 2)

How often do we mistake reluctance for lack of ability?

How many students are placed into experiences they did not choose—and quietly resist—only because they feel embarrassed, unprepared, or afraid to fail?

What happens when we interpret discomfort as disinterest, rather than as the beginning of growth?

This chapter is not about discovering talent.
It is about staying long enough for identity to form.

As educators, we are often quick to sort students into categories:

- "Motivated" or "unmotivated"
- "Talented" or "not musical"
- "Committed" or "checked out"

But many identities do not begin with passion.
They begin with proximity, access, and time.

Consider:

- What systems in your school allow students to opt out before they have had a real chance to grow?
- Where might embarrassment, financial barriers, or fear of failure be quietly shaping student behavior?
- Who decides when a student is "done" with a possibility?

Persistence is not always loud.
Growth is not always confident.
And commitment often develops after competence—not before it.

This chapter also reminds us of the power of adults who resist rushing the process.

One teacher who does not remove a student too quickly.
One counselor who encourages patience instead of escape.
One system that allows room for struggle without shame.

Sometimes the most important thing we can offer students is not inspiration—but permission to stay.

Stay when they are uncomfortable.
Stay when progress is uneven.
Stay when identity has not yet caught up with effort.

Because what a student becomes is not always what they intended.
Often, it is what they were allowed—quietly and consistently—to grow into.

3 The Road to Mastery (and What It Really Costs)

Core Question
What did my life teach me about excellence—and its price?

High School and the Expansion of Possibility

Music became my saving grace in high school.

The school I was originally zoned for had limited academic offerings and a reputation for gang violence. I was convinced—rightly or wrongly—that attending it would narrow my future. By that point, my growth on the trumpet had been rapid enough that my middle school band director encouraged me to audition for a newly opened performing arts magnet school: Dr. Michael Krop Senior High School.

I auditioned.
I was accepted.
My life changed.

Michael Krop was a world apart from anything I had previously known. I was used to outdated instruments and under-resourced programs. At Krop, the facilities were modern, the curriculum demanding, and the expectations unmistakably high. I performed regularly in concert band, jazz band, orchestra, and small ensembles. The instruments were new. The venues were polished—spaces my family could never have afforded to enter on our own.

For the first time, I was moving through environments that felt elevated—aspirational.

It was also the first time in years that I encountered a student body diverse not only racially, but economically. Admission was based primarily on audition and merit, not zoning. Students from vastly different backgrounds rehearsed, struggled, and performed side by side.

At the time, I didn't yet have language for why that mattered. I only knew that it did.

The Cost of Access

Ninth grade was where I developed the work ethic that still governs my life.

Because Krop functioned as a magnet school, I lived far from campus. Every morning, I woke up at 4:00 a.m. to navigate public transportation and catch the bus to school. Delays were common. Missed connections meant sprinting to make the next one.

I didn't think of this as hardship.
It was simply the cost of access.

And access felt worth it.

Excellence Without Protection

Looking back, ninth grade was also my first sustained encounter with harsh treatment within arts education.

One of my music directors—an older white man—frequently yelled at me and overlooked me for parts, despite strong performance. At the time, I did not frame this as racism. The thought never crossed my mind. I only knew that I was being treated more severely than others.

In retrospect, I sometimes wonder if I would have been treated differently had I looked different, or come from a different background.

I internalized more of that treatment than I should have. It stayed with me.

Still, ninth grade was largely successful. I was growing—musically and emotionally. That year, a mentor invited me to hear students from the New World School of the Arts perform.

I said yes without hesitation.

What I heard stunned me.

These were high school students—just like me—but the sound was professional, refined, and seemingly effortless. It was the most flawless ensemble playing I had ever encountered.

I learned that New World was widely regarded as the premier performing arts school in Miami-Dade County, housed on a college campus in downtown Miami. The school carried a mystique. Its commitment to artistic excellence was unmistakable.

From that moment on, I knew I had to be there.

Although New World rarely accepted students after ninth grade, I auditioned anyway.

I was accepted.

Living Inside the Art

At New World, academic coursework filled the mornings. The afternoons—from 1:00 to 4:00 p.m.—were devoted entirely to the arts.

- Wind ensemble
- Orchestra
- Jazz band
- Jazz combo
- Chamber music
- Brass techniques
- Music theory

We also received weekly private lessons—at no cost—from some of the finest musicians and educators in South Florida.

It was a pre-college conservatory experience, five days a week.

For the first time in my life, I had consistent private instruction.

Mastery and Its Uneven Terrain

While still in ninth grade, I began preparing for the Florida All-State Festival. At that point, I had no private teacher. My only guidance came from my middle school band director, who told me to practice each measure until it was mastered before moving on.

I took that advice literally.
Obsessively.

The auditions took place early in the school year. Roughly 300 trumpet players auditioned statewide. Only 20 to 25 were selected.

I was ranked second.

The achievement thrilled me—and unsettled me. I was proud, but deeply self-conscious. The only trumpet I owned was one my middle school director had given me, held together with Scotch tape. Because I had transferred schools, I had to return it. My family could not afford a replacement.

A friend from church loaned me his brand-new Bach Stradivarius for the festival. Nearly every other trumpet player owned the same instrument.

I earned All-State recognition in tenth grade.

Just a few years earlier, I had been among the weakest trumpet players in my middle school. Now I was being recognized as one of the strongest in Florida.

At the time, I didn't fully grasp the magnitude of that shift. I practiced not for accolades, but for sound—for process—for the quiet satisfaction of improvement.

One detail stands out in hindsight: out of approximately 125 students in the ninth- and tenth-grade All-State ensemble, only two were Black.

I didn't dwell on it then.
Later, it did come to mind.

New Stages, New Loss

That same year, New World welcomed a new jazz band director—ambitious, driven, and determined to elevate the program. He encouraged us to apply to Essentially Ellington, a national competition that invited only fifteen high school jazz ensembles each year.

We were accepted.

For me, this meant the possibility of meeting my idol, Wynton Marsalis, the festival's artistic director.

Once again, finances nearly intervened. My family could not afford the trip to New York. The school ultimately found funding—likely because I was a featured soloist on Duke Ellington's *The Shepherd*.

We traveled.
We competed.
We placed second.

During the final performance, Wynton Marsalis joined us on stage. I met him briefly—awkwardly—and I will never forget it.

Tenth grade ended triumphantly. I performed *Carnival of Venice* by J.B. Arban as a concert band soloist.

Music felt limitless.

Then, that summer, everything changed.

I was at a friend's house, and mentor tracked me down—no easy task in the days before cell phones—and told me he had a surprise.

I assumed it was a new trumpet.

Instead, he told me my father had died.

I laughed because I thought he was joking, this is my mind was inconceivable.

It wasn't a joke.

Carrying Excellence Through Grief

The shock was overwhelming. My mentor drove me home to my mother and sisters. We were devastated. My father, though emotionally distant, had provided stability. His death left us scrambling—not only emotionally, but financially.

We didn't even have enough money for his funeral.

My father died sick and broke.

That reality marked me permanently. I vowed my life would end differently.

My junior year was turbulent. I moved between relatives as my family searched for stability. Despite everything, I continued to perform at a high level.

That year, representatives from the Lake Luzerne Music Festival visited New World. I auditioned, was accepted, and received a 75 percent scholarship. The remainder was funded through professional work I took on.

Later, I participated in the Juilliard Experience, a program designed for underrepresented students. I received mentorship, lessons, and a glimpse of the life I wanted.

I knew then that New York City was my future.

By senior year, I was effectively on my own—academically, emotionally, and logistically. I slept on my sister's couch. I missed school due to exhaustion. Eventually, I was called into the principal's office to explain my absences.

I told the truth.

Against the odds, I graduated.

Music carried me through it all.

Closing Reflection

Excellence gave me access—to new schools, new cities, new stages.

But it also demanded a price: exhaustion, isolation, grief, and constant negotiation of belonging in spaces not built with me in mind.

I did not yet understand that mastery always comes with a cost.

I was simply paying it—
one note,
one bus ride,
one audition at a time.

Practice for Educators (Chapter 3)

Excellence is often celebrated without interrogation.

But achievement does not arrive equally.

Some students reach high standards with abundance behind them.
Others arrive there carrying instability, grief, scarcity, or exhaustion.

Ask yourself:

- How often do I praise outcomes without asking what they cost?
- What assumptions do I make about preparation, support, or ease?
- Who notices the student who excels quietly while carrying loss?
- Do my systems reward performance—or do they recognize effort as information?

This chapter is not an argument against rigor.
It is an argument for context.

When we celebrate excellence without understanding its price, we risk reinforcing inequity—even as we applaud success.

True educational leadership asks a harder question:

When students rise to our highest expectations, are we also prepared to rise to meet them—with attention, care, and responsibility?

Because mastery is not free.
And students should not have to pay for it alone.

4 Gateways, Mentors, and the Cost of Persistence

Guiding Question

What does it take to survive—and belong—in institutions that were never built with you in mind?

Rejection Season

By February of that year, auditions were behind me. Acceptance letters would begin arriving soon, and by May, everyone would know where they stood.

Juilliard was the first response I received.

The answer was no.

I wasn't surprised. I knew how that audition had gone. I accepted the result quietly and turned my attention to Manhattan School of Music—the school I truly hoped for.

Weeks passed.

Friends began receiving their letters. One by one, they were accepted to their dream schools, including MSM. I was the only one who hadn't heard back. The silence became unbearable. Eventually, I called the admissions office, hoping—naively—that someone might tell me my fate over the phone.

They couldn't.

Then the letter arrived.

Another no.

I was devastated.

I had applied to only two schools, and I had been rejected by both. By the time I considered the University of Miami, it was too late—the incoming class was already full.

I had no plan.
No safety net.
No clear path forward.

Scrambling for a Future

One option emerged out of necessity rather than desire: Florida Atlantic University, where my trumpet teacher from New World was on faculty.

The music program was small and in need of wind players—particularly for the marching band, which, to me, felt like a worst-case scenario. I had worked too hard to imagine my future circling a football field.

Still, I didn't have the luxury of preference.

The director of bands expressed strong interest. He told me he could guarantee admission, a full scholarship, and housing.

I considered it seriously.

Then came the caveat.

There was no housing available that year.

Instead, he offered something extraordinary: he invited me to live with him and his family.

I was close to saying yes—not because it felt right, but because it felt necessary.

Then something unexpected happened.

An Intervention

A famous trumpet and player who was a mentor from SUNY Purchase reached out to check in.

I told him the truth: I hadn't been accepted to either of my top-choice schools, and I planned to reapply the following year. My story moved him. He asked if I had considered SUNY Purchase.

I knew very little about the school—only that it was outside New York City but close enough to access it. That alone made it appealing.

He explained what I would need to do and recommended me to the classical department. He connected me with the trumpet professor.

We spoke by phone.

He asked me to prepare an audition via video recording—this was long before digital uploads—and mail it to him. I told him plainly that wherever I went, I would need a full scholarship. There was no college money.

I recorded the tape and sent it off.

Then I waited.

By that point, I desperately needed a win. I called repeatedly, asking whether the tape had arrived. Eventually, one day, it had.

He listened to it, and gave me encouraging feedback.

Not long after, he told me he wanted me at Purchase.

There was one condition: the full scholarship wouldn't be available until the following year.

I made my decision.

I would attend SUNY Purchase—and take a gap year.

Arrival at Purchase

When the gap year ended, I arrived at the SUNY Purchase Music Conservatory ready to work.

That first year was exhilarating and disorienting. One thing became clear quickly: I was a strong trumpet player. Other students asked why I was there, suggesting I was "too good" for the school.

I never felt that way.

I was simply grateful not to be a marching Owl at FAU.

I assumed I would study with the professor who had advocated for me. Instead, I was assigned to the studio of an adjunct faculty member—a respected freelancer and former student of a legendary orchestral trumpeter.

I didn't know him. I thought I would be put with the trumpet professor that I had been in contact with.
I felt blindsided.

Still, I adjusted.

I always did.

His expectations were uncompromising. Each week, he assigned roughly ten demanding items, all expected to be fully mastered by the next lesson—on top of ensemble rehearsals, chamber music, and academic coursework.

I was drowning.

At one point, he asked whether I had been a good student in high school—implying that I wasn't managing college well. It stung.

But I pushed through.

That year, I learned how far behind I truly was:

- Fifty orchestral excerpts
- Multiple etude transpositions
- Many pieces from the solo repertoire

I survived.

Being Seen

Midway through that year, the professor who had initially recruited me called me into his office.

He asked how I was adjusting.

Then he said something I couldn't process.

"We believe you have what it takes to become principal trumpet of the Chicago Symphony."

I dismissed it immediately. I assumed he was offering encouragement, nothing more. I had never seen anyone who looked like me in positions like that. I couldn't understand why he would say such a thing.

Later, I realized the truth.

He believed it.

From that moment on, my effort was being noticed.
Not just my sound—but my persistence.

The Cost of Staying

Despite artistic growth, the program was physically and emotionally demanding.

During my junior year, I was called into the brass chair's office and informed that I would lose half of my funding for not meeting performance expectations.

I was stunned.

But I reminded myself: I had one year left.

I would finish.

From that point forward, the professor who had recruited me became my sole teacher and primary influence. The summer before senior year, I worked, saved money, and practiced roughly three hours a day around my job.

At the start of my senior year I arrived at my first lesson nervous.

After I played, he said,

"With that sound, you could get into any orchestra."

I felt relief more than pride.

I wanted peace in my final year.

I served as principal trumpet in the college orchestra, presented a successful senior recital, and graduated from SUNY Purchase transformed as a musician.

Poverty in the Margins

There are realities of college life that rarely appear in success narratives.

Every semester, I received notices threatening housing removal or de-enrollment if my student fees weren't paid by a certain date. Each time, panic set in. I ran from office to office—Financial Aid, Accounts Payable, Housing—trying to keep myself enrolled.

Funding systems didn't communicate.
Aid arrived late.
Refund checks often came five weeks into the semester.

That meant no books.
No supplies.
No materials.

Some semesters, I began weeks behind—not because of laziness or neglect, but because I couldn't access what I needed.

Breaks were another challenge. I had no stable home to return to during holidays or summers. I rotated between friends' apartments, a cousin's couch—anywhere that would take me.

Stability was a luxury I did not have.

Between academics, trumpet practice, and survival logistics, college felt like competing in the Olympics.

I watched students from financially and emotionally stable homes drop out each semester.

I couldn't understand how.

I kept going.

Reflection: What It Took

College required far more than talent.

It required navigation—of systems, finances, expectations, and exhaustion.

I now understand that countless capable students—especially poor students and students of color—are filtered out not by lack of ability, but by attrition.

By burnout.
By silence.
By systems that mistake endurance for merit.

I am grateful I survived.

But survival should not be the price of education.

Practice for Educators (Chapter 4)

Talent does not fail in isolation.

It fails when systems demand endurance without support.

Ask yourself:

- Who gets to focus on learning—and who must focus on survival?
- How often do financial, housing, or bureaucratic barriers masquerade as "performance issues"?
- When students struggle, do we ask why—or do we simply record the outcome?
- Who intervenes when persistence is mistaken for weakness?

This chapter is not about lowering standards.

It is about seeing clearly.

Because when institutions reward only those who can endure invisible burdens, they mistake survival for excellence—and lose brilliance along the way.

5 Grit, Failure, and Reinvention

Core Question
What did my life teach me about resilience?

Playing at My Peak While the Ground Shifted

After completing my time at SUNY Purchase, I made a decision that surprised many people around me: I committed to a one-year service role with my church, working full-time in campus ministry.

On the surface, it looked like a sharp turn—from aspiring orchestral trumpeter to campus minister. But it wasn't a rejection of music, nor was it a permanent vocational shift. It was a season. A deliberate pause. A chance to deepen my faith, to serve students, and to better understand how belief, identity, and purpose intersected—both in my life and in the lives of others.

I never believed this role would replace music in the long term. I knew, quietly but clearly, that my path would return to performing and teaching. That tension hadn't resolved itself yet—but it wasn't lost on me either.

What made this period especially striking was this:

I was playing the best trumpet of my life.

By then, my training at Purchase had fully taken hold. Technically and physically, I felt complete. There was very little placed in front of me that I couldn't manage—major solo repertoire, principal orchestral excerpts, chamber music, commercial styles, salsa, and contemporary literature. I had range, endurance, flexibility, and confidence. The only areas where I felt less developed were lead trumpet and jazz improvisation—not because of limitation, but because I hadn't yet devoted sustained study to those idioms.

I was twenty-four years old, in peak physical condition, and artistically prepared.

Ministry work was demanding—full days of meetings, mentoring, planning, and teaching—but I protected my practice time fiercely. Somewhere between meetings and Bible studies, I carved out two to three hours a day to stay sharp. Trumpet practice wasn't optional; it was part of who I was, even in a season centered on service.

As an added gift, I was able to continue playing in ensembles at Purchase after graduating. That experience was pure joy. No grades. No juries. No pressure. Just music. I was playing simply to grow, to listen, and to be part of something larger than myself.

During that year, performance opportunities began appearing—often unexpectedly. Calls came from organizations I never imagined would reach out. Sometimes I didn't even know how they had my contact information. I had to decline a few opportunities due to work commitments, but each call confirmed something important:

My playing was moving in the right direction.

One of the most meaningful experiences from that period came through a brass quintet I performed with at Purchase. We were invited to serve as an ensemble-in-residence at the Bravo! Vail Music Festival in Vail, Colorado. Beyond our own performances, the festival offered proximity to the highest level of orchestral artistry. The New York Philharmonic and the Philadelphia Orchestra were among the featured ensembles that summer.

To rehearse, perform, and exist in the same artistic ecosystem as those musicians was grounding—and deeply affirming.

Vail itself was breathtaking. Even now, it remains one of the most beautiful places I have ever seen.

The Body Enters the Story

During this same period, there was an issue quietly unfolding—one I knew, vaguely, would return at some point, though I had no idea how profoundly it would affect my life.

Because of the instability and frequent movement of my childhood, regular dental care simply wasn't part of the picture. As a child, not going to the dentist felt like a win. Dentists weren't fun.

What I didn't understand was that playing trumpet on healthy gums is fun. Eating without pain is fun. Speaking clearly and confidently without obstruction—that's fun too.

As a working adult with health benefits for the first time, I began going to the dentist regularly. That felt like progress. Stability. Responsibility.

Then came the diagnosis.

I was told I had a genetic condition called juvenile periodontitis—a severe form of gum disease that causes rapid bone and tooth loss in young people. By the time it was identified, the damage to my lower front teeth was already extensive. The prognosis was blunt.

Those teeth could not be saved.

The recommended solution—dental implants with permanent prosthetics—was medically sound and financially devastating. The cost was approximately $20,000.

I didn't have that kind of money. I didn't even have a path toward it.

So the lower front teeth were removed and replaced with a temporary dental appliance—a functional placeholder rather than a true structural solution.

From a medical standpoint, it worked.
From an artistic standpoint, it changed everything.

The lower front teeth play a critical role in trumpet performance. They are part of the embouchure's anchor—the delicate balance of pressure, airflow, and muscular coordination that allows a brass player to produce sound with control and endurance. The temporary appliance didn't provide the same stability or feedback. It wasn't designed for professional brass playing.

And yet—by that point, I had developed enough efficiency, awareness, and technical control that I could still perform at an exceptionally high level. I adjusted. I compensated. I found new ways to balance what had been lost.

That still amazes me.

What this period revealed was not just resilience, but fragility—the reality that artistic excellence is shaped not only by discipline and access, but by the body itself. Musicians live inside their instruments. When something changes physically, the art must change with it.

I didn't yet understand how long this issue would linger—or how deeply it would shape my relationship with performance, identity, and sustainability.

I only knew something essential had shifted.

And I kept moving forward anyway.

Validation Without Safety

By the time a demanding brass quintet tour arrived—long rehearsals, exposed repertoire, no margin for instability—I was managing, but anxious. The tour would return us to Vail, performing alongside some of the finest orchestras in the world.

The first rehearsals were shaky. I felt exposed again— technically capable, physically uncertain. My embouchure didn't feel like home yet.

Still, I stayed with it.

When the tour arrived, I wasn't one hundred percent myself—but I was good enough.

After one particularly demanding piece, the principal trumpet of the New York Philharmonic turned to us and asked, "Was that you all playing that piece?"

When we said yes, he nodded and replied, "That sounded good."

I was playing first trumpet.

That moment mattered more than I let on at the time. The affirmation was quiet, professional, unembellished—and deeply meaningful. It told me that despite instability, despite physical change, the work was still speaking.

There were moments when the temporary appliance failed completely. More than once, it broke, and I had to crazy-glue it back together just to get through rehearsals or performances.

I made it through anyway.

Looking back now, it feels almost unreal.

What a wild ride.

When the Instrument Fell Away

Within the span of roughly two years, I moved from peak artistic form to physical instability, uncertainty, and a slow unraveling I couldn't explain.

After that tour—and in the year that followed—I was encouraged to pursue a master's degree. I wasn't particularly eager.

The year before, I had been waitlisted for Yale's master's program in trumpet performance. My interest in that program had less to do with prestige and more to do with one reality: it was free. When that option disappeared, I mentally closed the door on graduate school.

Then another opportunity surfaced.

I was offered the chance to return to Purchase with full tuition coverage. Given everything I was trying to navigate— financial stability, artistic direction, long-term sustainability— I decided to make it work.

At the same time, I was trying to do far too much: graduate school, a fledgling music school, a production company, continued ministry work.

No one sat me down and said, "This is too much." So I tried to do it all.

The result was predictable.

My first semester back at Purchase did not go well. The music school lasted eight months. The production company quietly dissolved. The reality of trying to build a life in the performing arts—especially without financial backing, generational support, or a safety net—hit hard.

Few people talk honestly about this.

Making a living in the arts is difficult under the best circumstances. Doing it while managing physical vulnerability, financial pressure, and institutional expectations—without a cushion—is exhausting.

I wasn't scattered because I lacked focus. I was scattered because I was trying to survive—artistically, musically, and economically—at the same time.

After my first semester back, I walked into my advisor's office knowing what I had to say—and dreading it. With regret and a great deal of fear, I told him I needed to withdraw from the program for personal reasons.

I felt ashamed admitting it.

I had been given an opportunity many people never receive, and I was walking away from it.

But I also knew the truth: I could not keep everything going at once. Something had to give.

When I walked out of that office, I was back at square one.

I needed a job—immediately. Rent, bills, food. The basic logistics of survival were nonnegotiable. There was no fallback plan and nowhere else to land.

So I did the only thing I could think to do:

I went looking for work.

I treated job hunting like a full-time job. I went to a large mall nearby and walked into what felt like every retail store—asking for applications, speaking to managers, following up. I wasn't being strategic. I was being urgent.

Eventually, I landed a job at Abercrombie & Fitch.

I won't dwell on that experience. It lasted about eight months, and that was long enough.

What I learned—again—was something I already knew about myself:

I have never done well in work that felt disconnected from who I am.

Jobs I didn't enjoy, I couldn't endure. I could show up for a while, but I couldn't stay. Each day in retail felt like time slipping away from me.

So I did something impulsive—and honest.

I walked back into SUNY Purchase and asked for my spot back.

I was accepted—but with a cost. The scholarship I had previously been awarded was gone. I no longer qualified for the same funding, and I knew that meant taking on more financial risk.

Still, it felt like a price worth paying.

I would rather struggle doing something that mattered to me than slowly disappear in a job that didn't.

Around that same time, something unexpected but important happened: I began working as a personal trainer.

Unlike retail, personal training fit me. It was physical, relational, and purposeful. I enjoyed helping people feel stronger and more confident in their bodies. While the income was too unstable to rely on full-time at that stage, it became an important supplement—and eventually, a lasting part of my professional life.

For a stretch, I worked seven days a week—either at Abercrombie or at New York Sports Club training clients.

It was exhausting, but it was forward motion.

And so there I was: back at Purchase, starting my master's degree for the second time, personal training to cover living expenses, and trying—once again—to balance survival with ambition.

It wasn't clean.
It wasn't easy.
But I was still moving.

Then something happened that I never saw coming.

Even though I was back at Purchase—and even though my playing had not dramatically declined immediately after my dental issues—my trumpet performance collapsed.

Almost overnight, I was operating at about fifty percent of my usual level.

I remember the day clearly.

I had taken my trumpet outside near the gym, a spot I liked because I enjoyed how the sound carried in the open air. I lifted the horn and played.

The sound was fuzzy. Unfocused. Resistant.

Above all, it was hard.

That was new.

Trumpet had not felt hard to me since middle school. Even during difficult periods, the instrument had always been something I could rely on.

Now, it felt foreign in my hands.

I went through every checkpoint I knew. I experimented with embouchure placement. I checked the horn and mouthpiece. I cleaned everything. I adjusted air, posture, approach—every technical solution I had ever learned.

Nothing helped.

It got worse.

I walked into lessons and was scolded as if I hadn't been practicing. The assumption was obvious: effort must be the issue.

After all, I had always been "one of the good ones"—the reliable player, the accomplished musician.

That identity evaporated quickly.

Colleagues grew distant. Teachers questioned my preparation. Peers stopped looking to me for leadership. Mentors watched quietly, unsure what to say.

It felt like living in a twilight zone—where everyone remembered who I had been, but no one knew what to do with who I was becoming.

The most disorienting part was this:

No matter how much I practiced, nothing improved.

That kind of helplessness is hard to describe unless you've lived it. It's like an athlete whose body suddenly refuses to respond, or someone whose entire identity is built around a skill that no longer shows up when needed.

For most of my life, I had been: Richard Fields—the trumpet player.

Now I was becoming something else: Richard Fields. He's struggling on the trumpet—but he's a good guy.

That distinction matters more than people realize—especially in classical music spaces. Being "nice" without being excellent is not currency. Respect, opportunity, and belonging are often tied directly to performance.

People had loved me because I was accomplished and kind. Remove the accomplishment, and the equation changes.

From that point on, my goal narrowed.

I no longer dreamed of thriving.

I just wanted to finish.

And I did.

But it was agony.

I was lost, disoriented, and grieving something I couldn't yet name. Still, somewhere beneath the frustration, I held onto a quiet belief:

Things would work out.

I just had no idea how.

Practice for Educators (Chapter 5)

Some students do not "lose motivation."
They lose stability.

Sometimes the issue isn't work ethic.
It's the body.
It's health.
It's grief.

It's money.
It's exhaustion.
It's the quiet collapse of a system they've been holding together with sheer will.

This chapter invites us to ask different questions—especially about high performers.

Ask yourself:

- When a student's performance changes suddenly, do I assume laziness—or do I investigate context?
- How often do I confuse capacity with character?
- Do my systems leave room for students who are dealing with invisible instability—health, housing, finances, family shifts?
- When someone is falling apart quietly, who notices before the consequences arrive?
- Do I treat resilience as a virtue—or as a signal that someone has been carrying too much for too long?

Most importantly:

What would it look like to meet struggle with curiosity instead of suspicion?

Not by lowering expectations.

But by widening our understanding of what it costs to keep going.

Because sometimes the strongest students are not the ones who need more pressure.

They are the ones who need someone to say:

"I see you. What's happening? And how can we stabilize this—together?"

6 When Effort Was No Longer Enough

Core Question
What happens when effort, excellence, and identity stop aligning?

Leaving Purchase, Entering the World

By the time I left Purchase, I was ninety-eight percent finished. In my mind, that meant done. I had one class left—just one—and I told myself I would return at some point to complete it. When or how didn't feel urgent.

What felt clear was this:

It was time to leave.

I needed to earn an income. I needed to figure things out.

Returning to Florida or Arizona to be closer to family wasn't really an option. There wasn't adequate space, and more importantly, I had built real connections in New York City—enough, at least, to believe I could make something work.

I had lived in Westchester County since my freshman year of college, where SUNY Purchase is located. When that chapter closed, I made the plunge into New York City.

A new environment.
A new energy.

The city felt alive in a way nothing else had—its smells, its noise, its relentless motion. By that point, I knew I had more than one skill I could rely on.

I could play trumpet—and teach it.
And I could train people.

The plan made sense. Personal training would provide stability. Trumpet would keep me connected to the professional music world. Fitness would support survival; music would sustain purpose.

For once, the idea didn't feel reckless.

It felt strategic.

Harlem, Hustle, and Holding the Line

When I moved into the city, I felt like I was on a clock. Things didn't just need to work out eventually—they needed to work out now.

I moved in with a friend from church in Harlem. The neighborhood wasn't the best, but it wasn't the worst either. We shared his studio apartment, and I slept on an air mattress that deflated every night. I would wake up pressed against the floor with crippling back pain. I remember thinking, half-joking, that this must be part of the cost of living in New York City.

I went back to work at New York Sports Club, this time at the Grand Central location. Surprisingly, I did quite well there. The pace was intense, but fitness once again gave me stability.

And somehow—despite physical issues playing trumpet—I was still getting work as a musician.

Even though I was nowhere near my peak as a player, I was playing well enough to secure lower-tier professional gigs around the city. I wasn't leading sections or being featured, but I was working. I even found myself performing at Carnegie Hall—more than once.

That alone felt surreal.

There were also a few orchestral tours scattered throughout that period. Nothing glamorous, but meaningful.

I was still practicing two to three hours a day. Progress was minimal, almost imperceptible—but I wasn't getting worse.

I had settled into a strange equilibrium:

No longer ascending, but not yet falling.

I was maintaining—and mistaking that for stability.

The Last Push

Eventually, I made a decision that felt both hopeful and desperate:

I was going to give the trumpet one final, honest attempt.

Even though I was no longer playing at my peak, I was still functioning at a respectable professional level by industry standards. I convinced myself that if I gave it one more full push—one last, uncompromising effort—I might reclaim a path toward orchestral trumpet playing.

Auditioning for an orchestra—any orchestra—is the musical equivalent of training for the Olympics. It demands total immersion. A relentless practice regimen. Often a coach. You eat, sleep, and breathe orchestral excerpts.

And the cost isn't just physical or emotional—it's financial:

Flights. Hotels. Meals. Rental cars. Time away from work.

These auditions are no joke.

When an audition for the Boise Philharmonic appeared, I jumped at it. My résumé was still strong enough to secure an invitation, and I wanted the job.

So I did what I had always done.

I worked hard.

I practiced three to five hours a day. I recorded obsessively. I analyzed, refined, rehearsed, sought feedback. I left no stone unturned.

When I boarded the plane to Boise, I was filled with anticipation.

I truly believed that effort—pure effort—would once again be enough.

The Audition

By that point, I hadn't taken many auditions. I had done a few in school and one or two professionally—none successful. I already (sort of) knew one thing:

Playing well and auditioning well are not the same skill.

Still, I arrived to the audition prepared.

I checked in early, warmed up carefully, and avoided overplaying. I sang excerpts. Centered sound. Stayed calm.

As the proctor walked me toward the audition space, I heard other trumpet players warming up.

If you're a trumpet player, you know this moment.

And what I heard stopped me cold.

These players sounded like living versions of orchestral excerpt recordings—centered, effortless, commanding. I remember thinking quietly, *The competition for Boise is serious.*

But there was nothing to do except walk in.

I played one round.

Five minutes, maybe less.

After the final excerpt, someone on the committee said, "Thank you."

And that was it.

What happened in those five minutes had little to do with preparation or musicianship.

It was a physical collapse.

Notes didn't speak. Attacks failed. Things either came out wrong—or didn't come out at all. It wasn't musical failure.

It was mechanical.

I remember thinking:

Three months of preparation for five minutes of unraveling.

I left the hall confused, frustrated, and deeply saddened. I boarded the plane back to New York carrying a small, irrational hope that somehow it might still work out.

It didn't.

But at the time, I didn't yet understand what that audition was really telling me.

When Effort Stops Working

The Boise audition didn't just mark a bad day.

It marked a shift.

Because for most of my life, effort had been reliable. If I practiced more, I improved. If I focused, I rose. If I sacrificed, the sacrifice eventually paid me back.

That was the bargain I believed in.

But now I was encountering a different reality:

Sometimes you can do everything right—and still lose the thing you built your identity around.

Not because you didn't work hard enough.

Because the body doesn't always negotiate.

And once that truth enters your life, you can't unlearn it.

The Shift That Created the Teacher

That audition didn't just end a dream—it clarified something I had been resisting for years.

I could still love the trumpet.
I could still work.
I could still grow.

But I could no longer build my future on the assumption that my body would cooperate the way it used to.

And that forced a new question:

If performance can disappear, what remains?

What remained was everything I had learned—about practice, discipline, fear, identity, pressure, survival, and the quiet emotional cost of trying to become excellent without a safety net.

For most of my life, I thought teaching was something you did alongside performing.

But now I began to see teaching differently.

Not as a backup plan.

As translation.
As transformation.

Because if I couldn't always rely on the instrument, I could still help someone else build a relationship with theirs—one rooted not just in achievement, but in resilience.

And slowly, without fanfare, I realized something I had not expected:

What I had survived might finally be useful.

That was the beginning of pedagogy.

Practice for Educators (Chapter 6)

This chapter is about a moment students experience all the time—but rarely have language for:

When effort stops producing results.

When doing "everything right" doesn't lead to the outcome they expected.

When identity and ability—once aligned—begin to drift apart.

As educators, we often reward the story we prefer:

Work hard and you will succeed.

And while that is sometimes true, it is not always true. There are real limits—physical limits, emotional limits, economic limits, systemic limits—that students run into long before we acknowledge them.

Ask yourself:

- When a student's performance stalls, do I assume a lack of effort—or do I consider hidden barriers?
- Do I treat "not improving" as failure—or as information?
- How do I support students when hard work doesn't produce the reward they believed it would?
- Am I teaching students only how to chase outcomes—or also how to live through disappointment without losing themselves?
- Do I create space for students to grieve lost identities—athlete, musician, honors student, "the smart one"—and still imagine a future?

Because what students often need in these moments is not a lecture.

They need guidance through a hard truth:

You can work with integrity and still not control the result.

And when that happens, the question becomes:

What remains of you—when the thing you've always been good at is no longer guaranteed?

This is where real maturity begins.

Not in winning.

In rebuilding.

And sometimes, the most powerful thing we can teach a student is this:

Your worth is not the same as your performance.
Your identity can expand.
And what you've survived can become wisdom—if you let it.

7 When Purpose Caught Up to Me

Core Question
What happens when the life you've been building can no longer ignore the work you're meant to do?

Taking Stock in New York

This period of my life felt like a pause—one of those rare moments where you look back long enough to see what you've survived.

There's an old saying: If you can make it in New York, you can make it anywhere.

By then, I was making it—not lavishly, but efficiently. I was doing okay.

I wasn't wealthy, but I was functional.
I had carved out a life.

I averaged between ten and fifteen performance engagements a year. Somehow, I always found work as a musician. I played well enough to stay employed, but not confidently enough to rely on music as my sole source of income. Music was still central to my identity—it just couldn't carry the full weight of my livelihood.

Personal training filled that gap.

I built steady income in fitness, including seasons in corporate roles. At one point, I had a strong clientele inside the gym and privately—private clients paying significantly more. That balance worked. Between training sessions, I could practice for multiple hours a day. My body stayed strong, my mind stayed focused, and my instrument stayed part of my daily rhythm.

The hardest part of fitness wasn't the work—it was the hours.

Early mornings. Late nights. Unpredictable schedules.

Still, the flexibility mattered. When performance opportunities arose, I could move sessions around and make the music happen. That adaptability allowed me to sustain both worlds.

I earned enough to support a modest life in the city. There were moments of real fear—times when I had almost no money to my name—but I survived those too.

And survival, by then, had become a skill.

I wasn't thriving the way I once imagined.
But I was standing.

And for a while, that was enough.

The Question I Could No Longer Avoid

Still, like many people at this stage of life, I wanted something more.

I wanted a partner.

And I think that desire—the desire to build a life with someone—was the catalyst I needed for clarity.

For years, friends and mentors had asked me about classroom teaching. Each time, I dismissed it immediately. To me, classroom teaching felt like an admission of failure—as if accepting a teaching role meant I hadn't "made it" as a performer.

That belief is common in our field.

And it is profoundly wrong.

There's an old, damaging adage that floats around the arts: Those who can't do, teach.

I wanted nothing to do with that narrative. I refused to let teaching be framed as a consolation prize, so I never allowed myself to seriously consider becoming an educator.

I would say things like:

"Teaching? Over my dead body."

Looking back now, I can say plainly: that was ignorance talking.

I remember a mentor—someone who genuinely believed in me—casually suggesting teaching as a possibility. I shut it down immediately, both internally and out loud.

Never, I thought.

That was my stance.

But time has a way of softening rigid beliefs—especially the ones built on ego.

Love Makes the Future Real

As I became newly engaged—happy, grounded, and building a future with my now wife, Samantha Fields—I could no longer avoid the larger questions.

I had to figure this out.

There were a few truths I could no longer ignore.

First: I knew I could not sustain a life doing work I disliked. That had never worked for me. It wasn't that I avoided effort—I worked relentlessly—but I could not justify spending my days traveling to a job I resented.

I stayed in fitness as long as I did because I genuinely enjoyed it, even though I knew, deep down, it was not my forever path.

Second: I knew there were two things I was deeply passionate about:

Music.
And helping people.

Up until then, those passions existed in parallel. I trained people. I played music. I cared deeply about both. But I had not yet imagined a life where they fully converged.

As my fiancée and I talked late into the night about the future—about stability, purpose, and the kind of life we wanted to build together—I came to a hard realization:

Four a.m. mornings followed by ten p.m. nights were no longer appealing—or sustainable—as a married man.

I had reached an intersection.

At that point, I held both a bachelor's degree and a master's degree in classical trumpet performance. I was a personal trainer who played professional trumpet gigs on the side. And I found myself asking, honestly and without ego:

What do I do with these degrees?
With these skills?
With these gifts?

For the first time, I didn't answer quickly.

I took a deep breath.

And I let go.

The only path that made sense—the only one that honored who I was becoming rather than who I had been trying to prove myself to be—was to stop running from teaching.

Not as a fallback.
Not as a failure.

As a calling.

Becoming Certified (and Becoming Serious)

With that decision made, I began the path toward becoming a K–12 music educator.

At first, I assumed the transition would be relatively straightforward. My only real concern was employment. All anyone ever seems to hear about arts education is that programs are being cut and jobs are disappearing. That narrative is loud—and persistent.

I remember exploring certification programs and asking one advisor, quite earnestly:

"Are there actually jobs in music education?"

Looking back now, I laugh at that question.

There are jobs. Plenty of them.

What there are fewer of are people prepared to do those jobs well—and to stay.

At the time, that clarity hadn't yet arrived.

I began sending out my résumé, attempting to secure interviews, only to confront a reality I had somehow delayed facing: if I wanted to teach in New York State, I would need to return to school—again—to earn certification.

Given my history, the thought of more school was deeply unappealing.

Still, the conclusion was unavoidable.

If this was the path forward, then I would do what was required.

So I enrolled in Brooklyn College's Advanced Certificate program in music education.

I quickly realized I was not the typical advanced certificate student.

Many of my peers were coming directly from undergraduate programs or performance-based master's degrees. While the cohort was diverse, I entered with years of professional performing experience, extensive work history, and a fully formed adult life already in motion.

I approached certification the way I approached work: seriously, pragmatically, and with intention.

In my mind, my performance in the program directly correlated to the kind of educator I would become. My grades weren't about academic validation—they were about professional accountability. I treated the program less like "school" and more like job training with real-world consequences.

That mindset made the logistics intense.

At the time, I was maintaining a full clientele at New York Sports Club, training private clients outside the gym, practicing, and adjusting to life as a newly married man.

Staying organized wasn't optional.

It was survival.

That period was exhausting.

But it was also clarifying.

For the first time, I could clearly see how my discipline as a performer—consistency, attention to detail, respect for process—could become a gift to students.

I wasn't just learning content.

I was translating a lifetime of practice into pedagogy.

The Internship Certificate: Betting on Myself

Layered on top of everything was a growing urgency:

I wanted a teaching job—now.

So desperately, in fact, that I began pursuing one before I had even completed certification.

At the time, New York State offered a pathway called the Internship Certificate—a provisional license that allowed individuals to teach full-time in New York City public schools while completing certification requirements.

There was one catch.

You had to convince a principal to hire you without being certified—on the promise that you would become certified once given the job.

In other words, you needed someone willing to take a risk.

So I hustled.

I worked relentlessly to get in front of principals. I attended school events. I networked aggressively.

In some cases, I even offered to play at school functions for free—something completely out of character for me.

I didn't play for free.
Not as a professional.
Not even as a teenager.

I had been paid for my performances since I was sixteen years old.

But I understood that this moment required a different calculation.

This wasn't about devaluing my artistry.

It was about opening a door.

I wasn't auditioning for a gig.

I was auditioning for a future.

Brooklyn: The Door Opens

Eventually, a friend recommended me to perform—again for free—at a school in Brooklyn: EBC High School for Public Service.

Up to that point, my experience with Brooklyn was limited. Most of my New York life had unfolded in the Bronx, Harlem, and Queens.

Brooklyn felt unfamiliar—new territory in a city I thought I already knew.

I met with the principal, who would later become both a friend and a mentor. I shared my desire to teach, to build an instrumental program, to create something meaningful for students who might not otherwise have access to music education.

Anyone who has worked in schools knows this truth:

Principals are among the hardest people to reach.

They are relentlessly busy, carrying responsibilities that rarely slow down.

So when he told me there might be a position opening—pending a few things—I tempered my excitement.

We went back and forth.

Then, finally, he told me there was a position.

And that I would need to interview.

I prepared the way I always do: thoroughly.

I built a complete program book outlining my vision—curriculum, ensemble structure, philosophy, and long-term growth. By that point, interviews didn't intimidate me. I hadn't done many, but I had been successful in every one I had.

I assumed this would be no different.

There was just one problem.

The principal I had built a relationship with wasn't present for the interviews.

Suddenly, the ground felt less stable.

My strongest advocate hadn't seen me teach, speak, or present. I had to trust that the hiring committee—people who didn't know my story—would see something in me.

And beneath it all was another truth:

I had never actually taught in a classroom before.

Three Rounds—and a Yes

The process unfolded in three rounds.

I passed the first.

Then came the demo lesson.

I taught the same lesson I had developed at Brooklyn College—structured, intentional, rooted in clarity and access.

It worked.

That lesson carried me into the third round.

Three candidates were brought in. We assumed there would be another task, another evaluation.

Instead, the administration offered all three of us the job on the spot.

I was elated.

It was one of the most gratifying moments of my life. I had secured a teaching position without yet holding full certification. There were still logistics to resolve, paperwork to complete—but once everything was finalized, I was issued an Internship Certificate and handed an official offer letter.

I was now a music teacher in the New York City Department of Education.

And just like that—

It began.

Practice for Educators (Chapter 7)

This chapter is a reminder that "calling" often arrives disguised as resistance.

Many future teachers do not reject teaching because they don't care about students.

They reject it because they're protecting an identity.

They're protecting a dream.
A narrative.
A version of success they believe they must prove.

So ask yourself:

- How many talented future educators have we lost because teaching was framed as "less than" performance?
- What messages do our institutions send—explicitly or subtly—about what counts as success in the arts?
- When someone says, "I could never teach," do we hear arrogance—or fear?

This chapter also names a practical truth about access:

Sometimes people are ready to teach before systems say they are "qualified."

That doesn't mean standards don't matter. They do.

But it does raise important questions:

- Do our certification pathways support strong candidates—or exhaust them?
- Who gets to "take the scenic route" into teaching, and who needs a faster on-ramp because life requires income now?
- When career-changers enter the profession with real-world experience, do we honor that strength—or treat them like anomalies?

And finally, this chapter points to a leadership question for administrators:

- Who are you willing to take a risk on?
- What do you look for when a candidate doesn't fit the traditional profile—but carries clarity, discipline, and purpose?

Because sometimes, the best educators aren't the ones who planned to teach from the beginning.

They're the ones whose life eventually made teaching unavoidable.

And when that happens—when purpose catches up—your job as an educator or leader is simple:

Open the door wide enough for them to walk through.

8 When the Fantasy Broke—and the Work Began

Core Question
What does teaching really demand when preparation isn't enough?

I got the job.

I was ecstatic. I truly believed I had arrived at the moment I'd been preparing for—even if I didn't realize it at the time. I could finally give back in the way others had given to me. I could pour into students the way mentors and teachers had poured into me. And if I was lucky—maybe just lucky enough—I could help shape the next generation's relationship with music.

In my mind, the dream had come true.

Now let me stop myself right there.

Because everything I just described sounds like the final scene of a movie—the triumphant ending, the credits rolling, the music swelling. And I need to be honest:

That fantasy could not have been further from the truth.

There was the fantasy.
And then there was the reality.

The fantasy looked like this: I walked into the classroom, trumpet in hand, and immediately connected with students. We played together. We jammed. I became their trusted adult, their mentor—the teacher who helped unlock their potential and guide them toward the beautiful world of music.

The reality was something else entirely.

I had no experience in New York City public schools.
I had no experience teaching—at all.
And I had almost no experience with general population students.

Since ninth grade, my educational life had existed almost entirely inside arts institutions—arts high schools, conservatories, colleges. I had spent years surrounded by students who had chosen music, who already believed it mattered.

The classroom I was walking into did not share that assumption.

Those two realities—my background and my students' world—weren't just different.

They were in direct opposition.

The First Day

My wife was excited. I was excited. Together, we believed I was stepping into something meaningful at EBC High School in Bushwick, Brooklyn.

One small but telling detail: I had to buy an entirely new professional wardrobe. Up until that point, most of my clothes were fitness gear and a few "Sunday best" outfits.

Suddenly, I needed to look like a teacher.

That should have been my first clue.

This wasn't just a new job.
It was a new identity.

I walked into the building on my first day with no idea what was about to happen.

By that point in my life, I would describe myself as thoughtful, reflective—and if I'm honest—relatively soft-spoken. I had never enjoyed being the center of attention. That worked just fine on stage with a trumpet in my hands.

In a classroom?

Not so much.

For any new teachers reading this, hear me clearly:

You will have to act.

This is your stage.

You will need to speak louder than feels natural.
Think faster than feels comfortable.
Occupy more space than you're used to.

I watched my colleagues at EBC with awe. They commanded rooms effortlessly. Students listened. They could quiet what felt like a football stadium with sheer presence alone.

And there I was thinking:

What am I doing here?

The students didn't help my nerves.

Many of them were physically bigger than me. In my eyes, they looked like giants. And professionally speaking, that first day may have been one of the most intimidating moments of my life.

Here's the irony that still makes me laugh.

I had played solo trumpet in front of crowds of twenty thousand people.

That didn't scare me.

Standing in front of these students?

Terrifying.

Not because of them. They were good kids—curious, energetic, human.

The fear was internal.

Would they listen to me?
Could I actually help them?
What happens when they realize I don't know what I'm doing?

I stood there holding a title I had worked relentlessly to earn—teacher—while quietly wondering if someone was about to tap me on the shoulder and say,

"Sorry. We made a mistake."

That was my real first day.

And that was the beginning of my actual education.

When the Lesson Failed

What I've described so far was only the beginning of the day—students lining up outside the classroom.

What happened next will either make you laugh, terrify you, or both.

I used the same lesson on my first day that I had used during my demo lesson interview. I didn't have anything else prepared, and at the time, it felt like the safest choice.

I would introduce myself.
Share my story.
Play some music.
Invite students to experience music emotionally.

It had worked once.

It did not work again.

I greeted students warmly at the door. About half acknowledged me. The rest walked straight past—some with expressions that, in my nervous state, felt closer to snarls than indifference.

The lesson didn't land.

Students talked over me.
Ignored me.
Dismissed me.

When I picked up the trumpet—my most reliable source of authority for my entire life—the reaction shocked me.

They laughed.

"You suck."
"That thing is loud—shut up."

Music, which had always commanded respect elsewhere, meant nothing in this room.

At one point, another adult in the room—a paraprofessional—tried to help. Seeing me struggle, they shouted at the top of their lungs:

"SHUT UP!!!"

The room went silent.

For about forty-five seconds.

Then the noise returned.

Moments later, a student walked up to me and shouted,

"You are one of the most brolic music teachers I've ever seen."

Then he yelled,

"F— this, I'm out!"

And walked out.

The class erupted in laughter.

That was my first day of teaching.

No Exit Plan

By the end of the day, I was exhausted—physically, mentally, emotionally. I questioned everything.

This was rough. Rougher than auditions. Rougher than rejection. Rougher than financial stress.

Before that day, I had made a pact with myself:

No matter what happens, you do not quit teaching.

No exit plan.
No quiet escape.
No alternate story where this "wasn't really for me."

Standing there after that first day—shaken and humbled—I clung to that pact.

Because if I had given myself an out, I would have taken it.

Building What Didn't Exist

The first semester—the first four months—was brutal.

I had been hired to build a music program from scratch. And "from scratch" doesn't fully capture it.

There were no instruments.
No music room.
No curriculum.
No inherited culture.

And no margin for failure.

If the program didn't take hold, my contract wouldn't be renewed. I wasn't just teaching.

I was auditioning every single day.

The first thing I learned was this:

Before I could teach music, I needed culture.

Not classroom management—classroom culture.

Students aren't employees.
They aren't problems to control.
They are young people placed in our care.

Culture is the invisible architecture that determines whether learning can happen at all.

Once culture began to take shape, a new challenge emerged:

How do you actually teach instruments during the school day?

I taught in four different spaces—none designed for music. I secured a small grant to purchase starter instruments. That win mattered.

It meant the program was real.

I applied for grants relentlessly. I attended workshops. I pivoted constantly.

At first, I taught Afro-Latino music history. The content mattered—but students weren't making music.

They were learning about music, not doing music.

So I pivoted again.

I built beginning ensembles. Guitar. Piano. Percussion. Even recorder—imperfect, but functional.

One student wrote in anonymous feedback:

"I hate playing the recorder with all of my heart."

I laughed—then listened.

That feedback wasn't disrespect.

It was data.

The End of the First Year

By the end of the year, we had built something real.

A choir.
Performances.
Students on stage making music—some for the first time in their lives.

There were many days I didn't feel capable.

But I showed up anyway.

Progress didn't happen in comfort.

It happened in consistency.

That first year nearly broke me.

And it clarified everything.

I made it through without quitting.

More importantly, I made it through without being fired.

When the year ended, I wasn't confident.

But I was prepared.

I was no longer a first-year teacher.

I had begun becoming a pedagogue.

Practice for Educators (Chapter 8)

This chapter is a reminder that inspiration is not a strategy.

Many new teachers enter the classroom with a beautiful idea of who they want to be:

The mentor.
The motivator.
The artist who changes lives.

But students don't meet our intentions.

They meet our presence, our systems, and our consistency.

Before we ask, "How do I make them love this?" we may need to ask a more honest question:

Have I built a classroom where learning is even possible?

Consider:

- Do I confuse a strong lesson with a strong culture?

- Do I assume students will value what I value—or do I teach them why it matters?
- When something fails, do I interpret it as disrespect—or as information?
- Have I built routines that protect instruction, or am I relying on personality and volume?

This chapter also invites a deeper truth:

Teaching is not primarily about performance.
It's about containment.

Can you hold a room?
Can you hold students' attention without humiliating them?
Can you hold your own emotions when you feel exposed?

And when your "best plan" collapses in real time, can you keep your dignity long enough to learn?

Because the first year is rarely about mastery.

It's about survival with integrity.

And what separates teachers who grow from teachers who leave is often one decision:

Will I treat failure as proof I don't belong—
or as part of the training?

Sometimes, the classroom doesn't break us because we're not called.

It breaks the fantasy so the real work can begin.

And if we stay—if we learn—if we build culture before we chase excellence—

we don't just become teachers.

We become practitioners.

We become steady.

We become the kind of adult many students have been waiting for.

9 Teaching Across Contexts: What the Work Revealed

Core Question

What does the work reveal when you teach long enough—and in enough places—to stop romanticizing any one version of it?

Opening: After the First Year

One of my administrators used to repeat a familiar adage:

"It's always easier after the first year."

With distance and perspective, I don't disagree—but I also don't accept it at face value.

It's true that you will never experience another first year of teaching. In that sense, the statement holds. The first year is singular. It is a landmark period—like the first year of marriage, the first year of parenthood, or the first year of any role that fundamentally reshapes who you are. There is no rehearsal for it. No shortcut around it.

That first year challenged me in ways I had never experienced before—neither as a child nor as an adult. In earlier seasons of my life, the difficulties I faced were sometimes the result of my own choices, and sometimes circumstances beyond my control.

This experience was different.

It was uniquely formative.

And when I say formative—or even positive—I want to be precise about what I mean.

Positive does not mean pleasant.
It does not mean I walked into school each day feeling joyful, confident, or affirmed.
There were no metaphorical roses. No carefree moments.

What made that year positive was this simple truth:

Without it, I would not truly understand teaching, myself, or who I am within teaching.

That year gave me clarity I could not have arrived at any other way.

What I came to realize, however, is that while the first year is singular, every year brings its own form of challenge. Even as I became more competent—more efficient, more confident, more skilled—the work continued to demand growth. Each year asked something new of me.

Sometimes the challenge was understanding students more deeply.
Sometimes it was understanding myself.
Sometimes it was navigating colleagues, systems, families, and shifting expectations.
And sometimes it was wrestling with pedagogy itself—what works, what doesn't, and why.

I never felt as though I had "arrived."

And I'm grateful for that.

I've always been drawn to the phrase teaching practice—not because teaching should ever be taken lightly (it is a serious vocation), but because the word practice implies humility, reflection, and continual becoming.

We are never finished.
We are always learning.

And the moment we stop growing in our practice is the moment we should begin asking difficult questions—not about our students, but about ourselves. About our assumptions. Our habits. Our willingness to change.

Because when growth stops, the people most affected are not us.

It's the students.

Section 1: Teaching in the NYC Department of Education

The Work That Made Me Durable

After that first year, I was able to sustain and carry forward another five years of program building—years that would prepare me for virtually any arena I would later enter in my career.

When the first year ended in Brooklyn, the work was far from finished. The program still needed structure. I still needed a dedicated space. I needed more instruments. I needed to deepen and normalize an instrumental music presence within the school.

What had changed, however, was perception.

By the second year, both students and staff understood something important:

I wasn't going anywhere.

I was serious. I was invested. And I believed deeply in what we were building together.

That second year, I felt more confident—not just in my teaching, but in myself. I no longer questioned whether I belonged in the room.

I knew I had something meaningful to offer my students.

And I also knew this:

I wasn't simply teaching music.

I was teaching life.

I cared deeply about students' growth as musicians—but even more, I cared about who they were becoming as people. Somewhere along the way, I realized that music was not the end goal.

Music was the vehicle.

It was the language through which I could reach them, challenge them, affirm them, and help them see themselves differently.

This was the moment I fully adopted a belief that still guides my work today:

Teaching the human far outweighs teaching the content.

Now let me be clear about what I mean—and what I don't mean.

This philosophy did not lead me to take music or music education less seriously. On the contrary, I began taking my craft more seriously than I ever had before. I practiced not only my primary instrument, but the instruments I taught—guitar, bass, piano, percussion, band instruments, voice—everything. I worked relentlessly to deepen my fluency.

Why?

Because content mastery is credibility.

Music was my vehicle. And the more seriously I took the content, the more seriously students took me. When care and consistency were paired with real expertise, trust followed.

That combination mattered.

When I could say, "I played at Carnegie Hall," or "I toured internationally," or "I performed with professional orchestras," it wasn't about status.

It was about alignment.

When students saw that excellence lived alongside care—alongside genuine belief in them—the impact multiplied.

Over the next five years, I secured more than $150,000 worth of instruments. I established beginner, intermediate, and advanced band programs, along with guitar classes. I partnered with an exceptional colleague, **Paula Brion**, to build and sustain a vocal ensemble. I brought in outside dance companies and teaching artists to work with students.

Because I knew something deeply—and without question:

Students don't just need access to the arts.
They need access to the arts at a high level.

They need to learn from accomplished artists and committed educators.

There's a phrase that circulates far too casually in our field:

"Those who can't, teach."

I reject that outright.

Continued growth should never detract from artistry. It should enhance it. Teaching is not the absence of excellence—it is one of its most demanding expressions.

What those years taught me—beyond curriculum, beyond logistics, beyond program building—was this:

When artistry, rigor, care, and belief align, education becomes transformative.

Not just for students.

For teachers too.

Section 2: Teaching in the Suburbs

When Context Exposed the Truth

As life unfolded, the demands of my family and the broader trajectory of my life led me into the next chapter of my teaching career.

Leaving Brooklyn required walking away from something I deeply loved: the students, the community, and the program I had built from nothing. With the exception of my faith, my marriage, and my trumpet, there are few commitments in my life that demanded as much of me as those years in New York City public schools.

Because of changing family circumstances—and a growing desire to be more present for my spouse and young child—I made the difficult decision to accept a middle school band position closer to home.

It was necessary.

And it was heartbreaking to leave Brooklyn.

I stepped into a position in a small suburban district in Connecticut, one rooted in a strong musical tradition. In contrast to everything I had just experienced, the program was fundamentally different from the one I had left.

Where my Brooklyn program began with no instruments, no room, and no infrastructure, this school had a long-standing tradition of music education. There was a large, dedicated band room. There were ample instruments. Many students owned or rented their own instruments. Some had received music instruction in elementary school.

The foundation already existed.

This shift forced me to confront something important:

Context matters—far more than we often admit.

Before I arrived, many people warned me about middle school.

"Run," they said.

That was not my experience.

Yes, middle school students were navigating adolescence.
Yes, they were impulsive and emotional. But they were also
curious, open, and willing to explore. They were still
children—and that mattered.

Compared to my high school students in the city, these
students carried less emotional weight into the classroom.
Their challenges were real—but not compounded by the
same degree of instability. Academically, many were already
ahead of where my urban high school students had been at
the same age.

This observation unsettled me—in the best possible way.

I want to be clear:

This is not a comparison of who has it better or worse.

It is an observation about conditions.

Consider a typical morning for one of my students in New
York City: a crowded apartment, public transit filled with
exhaustion and unpredictability, an overcrowded school,
inconsistent staffing, and responsibilities far beyond their
years.

Now contrast that with my suburban setting: stable housing,
predictable routines, school buses, spacious facilities, and
broad access to arts and academic programs.

These differences are not about motivation or ability.

They are about atmosphere, access, and resources.

For the first time, I felt truly set up for success.

That didn't make the work easy.

It made the work possible.

Teaching in both environments reshaped how I understand education as a whole. Each setting demanded something different. Each revealed different truths.

Together, they gave me a fuller picture of what educators are actually navigating—and why context cannot be ignored.

Section 3: Teaching in Higher Education

From the Classroom to the Conservatory—and Back Again

Because this book is about my journey as an educator, it feels important to speak honestly about my experience in higher education.

While teaching K–12, I began my second master's degree in music and music education at Teachers College, Columbia University. This decision was not incidental. Long before I entered a classroom, I had carried the idea of earning a doctorate. Once I committed to teaching, that desire returned—with clarity.

Teachers College took a chance on me—but not all the way.

I was admitted into the master's program, not yet the doctoral program I hoped to enter.

I understood the message clearly:

Prove it.

So I did.

I approached scholarship with the same intensity I once gave trumpet practice. I prepared relentlessly. I rewrote constantly. I treated feedback seriously. I showed up.

That effort paid off.

I was admitted into the Doctor of Education (Ed.D.) in the music and music education program at Teachers College. Upon entering the program I was named a Florence K. Geffin Scholar. When I received that news, I cried. It represented the fulfillment of a ten-year dream carried through reinvention, failure, and persistence.

As I write this, I have been "Dr. Fields" for over a year.

That journey opened the door to higher education—not as a departure from K–12 teaching, but as a continuation of it.

At the time of writing this, I serve as a Visiting Assistant Professor of Music, a Pep Band Director, and an Applied Instructor.

Before I began teaching at the college level, I asked myself honestly:

Will I be any good at this?

College students aren't looking for perfection.

They're looking for alignment.

They watch closely to see whether you practice what you preach. They challenge ideas not to resist—but to engage.

Higher education is not easier than K–12 teaching.

It is different.

Each environment asks something unique of the teacher. But the work remains the same at its core:

When learning clicks—for a child, a teenager, or an adult—it is equally powerful.

After all, pouring into others—

Isn't that what this teaching thing is all about?

Practice for Educators (Chapter 9)

This chapter is a call to stop oversimplifying teaching.

Not because teaching is too complex to understand—
but because oversimplification hides what's actually shaping student outcomes: context.

Ask yourself:

- Do I confuse student motivation with student conditions?
- When a student struggles, do I assume a deficit in character—or a deficit in support?
- Do I recognize how much my own success depends on systems I didn't create but benefit from?
- Am I building my practice in a way that can travel across contexts—or only succeed in one?

This chapter also challenges a myth many educators carry—
quietly or unconsciously:

"If I'm good enough, it should work anywhere."

But good teaching isn't magic.

It's not immune to staffing shortages, overcrowding, poverty,
trauma, instability, or inequitable access.

So here's the deeper question:

What does it mean to be excellent and honest about
conditions?

Because students don't need our saviorism.

They need our clarity.

They need educators who can say:

This is hard—and it makes sense that it's hard.
You're not broken. The system is under-resourcing you.
We will still work. We will still grow. And we will tell the
truth while we do it.

Finally, consider this:

Every time you teach in a new context—
you're not just learning about students.

You're learning about what your systems reward.
What your systems ignore.
And what your students are being asked to overcome just to
show up.

And once you see that clearly, the work changes.

You become less judgmental.
More strategic.
More humane.

And in the long run, that may be the difference between a
teacher who "works hard"—
and a teacher who actually makes things better.

10 The Art Within the Teacher

Core Question
How does a life—fully lived—become a teaching practice?

Teaching Is Not Just Technique

Now that I have shared my life, my teaching, and my music, I want to step back and name what all of it is pointing toward.

Each experience—on stage, in classrooms, in rehearsal rooms, and in moments of uncertainty—quietly shapes who I am when I teach, when I perform, and when I stand before others to speak. Whether one believes in fate, divine calling, vocation, or simple happenstance, one truth feels undeniable to me:

Our lived experiences form us.
They shape how we listen.
How we respond.
How we lead.
How we care.

None of this happens in isolation.

My musicianship informs my teaching.
My teaching refines my artistry.
My failures clarify my values.
My perseverance sharpens my empathy.

Over time, these threads braid together into something cohesive—not perfect, but honest.

What follows is not a formula.
It is not a checklist.
And it is certainly not a prescription.

It is a reflection—an offering.

I invite you into my heart and mind as I share the pathways that continue to help me become my best self—not only in the classroom, but on the stage, and in any space where leadership, connection, and purpose matter.

Take what resonates.
Leave what doesn't.
And consider how your own story may already be shaping the teacher, artist, or leader you are becoming.

The Art Within the Teacher

I still hear—again and again—that teaching and music-making are somehow diametrically opposed. That choosing one means sacrificing the other.

I see the quiet grief that belief can carry.

I witness educators who, unable to fully live out their dreams as orchestral musicians, rock artists, or opera singers, throw themselves completely into the classroom while quietly leaving behind the very thing that brought them there in the first place:

musicking itself.

I want to be clear.

I am deeply opposed to this idea.

Not out of judgment—but out of conviction.

Because if I am asking students to love something, to take
risks within it, to invest themselves fully in it, that invitation
must come from a place of genuine engagement within me.

Passion cannot be outsourced.
Belief cannot be performed convincingly without truth
behind it.

This does not mean every educator must perform relentlessly
or sacrifice rest and sustainability. That is neither healthy nor
wise.

But it does mean this:

I believe I must remain alive—mentally, emotionally,
creatively—in my relationship with music.

I do not believe I have the right to ask students to care deeply
about music unless it is still pouring out of my own bones.

Because disconnection leaks.
Unfulfilled potential speaks—even in silence.
Students feel it.

For me, this belief takes practical form. On classroom breaks,
I play—trumpet, trombone, flute, guitar, oboe, keyboard.
While lesson planning, I listen constantly—to my own
ensembles, to professional recordings, to the sounds I want
my students to imagine and embody.

Music is never something I teach and then put away.
It is something I live inside.

And something unexpected keeps happening.

As I stay deeply connected to my artistry, performance
opportunities continue to appear. Teaching, performing, and
musicking do not compete—they reinforce one another.

The more seriously I take my art, the more grounded my
teaching becomes.
The more intentional my teaching, the more honest my
playing feels.

And my students know.

They sense when I am growing.
They sense when I am striving.
And if I were to stop, they would sense that too.

My impact in the classroom does not come despite my
commitment to artistry.
It comes because of it.

How Life Teaches Me to Teach

What gives lived experience power in teaching is not the
experience itself—it is how that experience is translated.

What many would label hardship, instability, or struggle
becomes, over time, quiet strength. Those moments teach me
how to lead when certainty is unavailable. That ability gives
me authority in the classroom long before I have language for
it.

And as I reflect, there are a few core beliefs—few essential postures—that carry me, shape me, and continue to guide me.

Adapting to Change

One of the most difficult skills for people to embrace is adaptation.

Even now, I sometimes fight change with everything in me. We grow attached to routines, to predictability, to knowing what comes next. Comfort is seductive.

But life does not honor comfort.

Early on, I learn—often without choice—that change is not optional. Circumstances shift. Environments evolve. Stability is never guaranteed.

And because of that, I learn something essential:

Resistance delays movement.

So I adapt. I adjust. I keep going.

That skill follows me into the classroom.

When initiatives change.
When schedules shift.
When students arrive carrying invisible weight.
When progress is uneven and behavior unpredictable.

I learn to respond rather than react.

Adaptability is not weakness.
It is leadership.

Education is dynamic. It asks us to pivot constantly. My very first day of teaching is nothing but micro-adjustments— moment after moment of recalibration. No script. No control. Only presence.

If you want to have impact—in teaching or in life—you must be willing to embrace change.
Not resentfully.
Not fearfully.
But with courage.

The classroom does not reward rigidity.
It rewards responsiveness.

Persisting Through Difficulty

One of the defining skills that sustains me—especially early on—is persistence.

This matters more than we often acknowledge.

Many educators leave the profession before five years not because they lack care or intelligence, but because the difficulty overwhelms their expectations. Teaching is emotionally demanding, relationally complex, and relentlessly human.

For me, persistence is not new.

Years of poverty, unstable living situations, and the unforgiving world of classical music already teach me how to endure discomfort without abandoning purpose.

Difficulty does not signal failure.
Difficulty signals meaning.

When teaching feels overwhelming, I do not interpret struggle as a sign to leave. I understand it as part of the work.

Difficulty is not a disqualifier.
It is the terrain.

Those who thrive are not the ones who avoid struggle, but the ones who learn how to remain present long enough for growth to occur.

Striving to Be My Best (Without Needing to Be Perfect)

From my earliest struggles with the trumpet to my work today, one principle continues to guide me:

Show up fully.
Not perfectly.
Not comparatively.
Honestly.

Striving to be your best does not mean having your best day every day. It means refusing to cut corners. It means doing what you know you should do—even when no one is watching.

There is no free lunch.

What we avoid always shows up when it matters most—on the concert day, on the observation day, on the day the student finally tests whether you mean what you say.

This mindset does not guarantee ease or recognition.

What it guarantees is integrity.

Presence beats perfection every time.

Being Curious—and Always Learning

Curiosity is non-negotiable.

Experience without curiosity hardens into assumption. And assumption is where we begin losing students—quietly.

I do my best work when I put on my researcher's hat: when I listen before I act, observe before I judge, and ask better questions than the ones my instincts want to ask.

Curiosity creates space for understanding.
Understanding creates space for growth.

For students—and for us.

A Deep Care for Others

I learn early that the world is unequal—and that people carry more than we can see.

Long before teaching, I am drawn toward care: listening, helping, investing. I bring that into the classroom.

Let this land plainly:

If you do not love people—and if you do not care deeply for children—you must confront that before entering teaching.

Care is not softness.
It is not weakness.

It is the foundation that allows rigor to exist without harm.

Students know when they are genuinely cared for.
You know when you are leading with love.
And the room knows too.

Teaching without care becomes hollow.
Teaching with care becomes sacred.

Closing: Becoming

This journey—of sharing my life and my teaching—lives
within me still, like the fire the prophet Jeremiah could not
contain.

Writing this book is not about conclusions.
It is about truth.

And if there is one thing I hope you take with you, it is this:

Your story is not separate from your practice.
It is already shaping it.

Every loss.
Every transition.
Every hard season.
Every quiet victory.

It is all becoming something.

My hope is that you—educator, artist, leader, or seeker—will invite your heart and mind into the work of becoming your best self.

Not someday.
Not when circumstances are ideal.
Right where you are.

Always seek to do good.
Be patient with others.
Be kind in your actions.
And extend that same grace to yourself.

Because growth is not linear.
Purpose is rarely obvious in the moment.
And becoming—whether in the classroom, on the stage, or in life—is a lifelong practice.

And that may be the most meaningful work we are ever given to do.

Practice for Educators (Chapter 10)

Before you try to "improve" your teaching, ask a deeper question:

Am I still alive inside the work?

Because students don't just learn content.
They absorb posture. Presence. Energy. Integrity.

Reflect:

- Where have I become disconnected—from my art, my curiosity, or my sense of purpose?

- What part of my craft do I need to re-enter—not for applause, but for alignment?
- Do my students see me growing in real time?
- When change arrives, do I resist—or do I respond with steadiness?
- When difficulty comes, do I interpret it as failure—or as terrain?
- Do I lead with care strong enough to hold both rigor and dignity in the same room?

Then make one small commitment:

Choose one practice this week that makes you feel alive again.
One recording you return to.
One passage you refine.
One conversation you have with curiosity instead of assumption.
One moment you notice a student carrying more than they can name.

Because your greatest teaching tool isn't your lesson plan.

It's the life you bring into the room.

And when your life and your practice align—
students don't just learn.
They become.

PRINCIPLES MADE VISIBLE: THREE CLASSROOM STORIES

What Happens When Conditions Align

I felt it was both prudent and responsible to share how these principles have shown up not only in my own life, but in the lives of students I have had the privilege to teach. I knew teaching would be a journey—but no one prepared me for how profoundly I would be changed by witnessing growth, agency, and transformation in real time.

Over the course of my career, I have taught thousands of students across multiple contexts. There are too many stories to tell. The ones shared here stand out not because they are extraordinary in isolation, but because they reveal what becomes possible when access, belief, structure, and care align.

All student names and identifying details in the following accounts are pseudonyms, used to protect privacy. The stories themselves, however, are real. They reflect lived moments in classrooms——moments that reshaped how I understand potential, learning, and my responsibility as an educator.

Marcus: When Access Revealed Ability

Marcus was an eleventh-grade student—quiet, unassuming, and socially adept in ways that suggested careful self-management. He carried a confidence that was intentional, almost guarded. It became clear to me early on that he was highly capable, but equally committed to keeping those capabilities hidden. Excellence, for him, came with social risk.

Marcus was one of the first students I ever taught in a K–12 setting. His story remains singular in my memory because I had never encountered anything quite like it before—and I haven't since.

In my early years of teaching, resources were minimal. I had little equipment and no inherited program to lean on. Through persistent advocacy, I eventually secured a small set of electronic keyboards—about fifteen in total. I designed one class as a kind of musical laboratory: a space where students could explore guitar or keyboard freely, pursue their own musical interests, and learn through experimentation rather than prescription.

At that point, many of my students were academically and musically below expected grade-level benchmarks. I never understood this as a deficit in them. I understood it as evidence of something missing in their educational paths—access, exposure, opportunity. I never believed they needed to be "fixed." I believed they needed room.

For many students, this class marked the first time they had ever held an instrument. The level of engagement was immediate and sincere. There was a kind of purity in the room—students learning not for grades or approval, but out of curiosity and joy.

One day, I handed Marcus a keyboard.

Without any prior piano experience or formal training, he opened YouTube, found a recording of Beethoven's *Für Elise*, and began teaching himself the piece. As I watched, he learned the first twenty measures on his own—during class.

At first glance, it appeared he was off task. He was not following the assigned method book. He wasn't working through the prescribed exercises. I had that concern—briefly.

But the reality was this: Marcus had already surpassed the material in the curriculum. He had taken ownership of his learning and pushed himself well beyond the assignment—without prompting, without praise, and without a piano at home. This is simply what he chose to do with the time and access he was given.

That moment challenged everything I thought I understood about learning, progress, and human potential. My own musical development had been built on years of disciplined practice and incremental growth. What I witnessed that day was something different: intense focus, limited time, and unmistakable musical giftedness emerging the moment opportunity appeared.

From that point forward, I stopped questioning what students could or could not do.

My responsibility became clear: to create the conditions for learning, and then to pay close attention when students showed me where instruction needed to go. What we now describe as student-centered learning or a constructivist approach was not a pedagogical trend for me—it was a lived realization.

That day changed both of us.

Ashley: When Music Became a Place to Belong

Ashley was a tenth-grade student—soft-spoken, consistently kind, and almost always smiling. She never caused problems in my class. She followed directions, participated quietly, and moved through the room with a kind of gentle attentiveness that rarely draws attention.

What I didn't initially understand was how differently she was perceived elsewhere.

Colleagues would occasionally stop me in the hallway and say things like,
"Wow, Ashley is really struggling in my class," or
"She has significant behavioral issues," or
"She's very low academically."

Each time, I was confused.

The student they described did not resemble the student I knew.

This is one of the quiet gifts of teaching in the arts—though I believe the insight applies to every subject. In my classroom, I rarely encountered the behaviors other teachers reported. Not because they weren't real, but because context matters. When students are placed in environments where they feel competent, valued, and seen, different versions of them emerge.

With Ashley, I began noticing something subtle but consistent.

She lingered.

She came to practice her brass instrument during lunch— initially alone, without prompting. Over time, she stayed longer. Then she began helping other students. What started as private persistence slowly became quiet leadership.

123

No one assigned her this role.
She claimed it.

Before music, I'm not sure how much Ashley had to look forward to during her school day. That realization didn't come all at once—it unfolded slowly. Watching her in the band room, I began to understand that music was not just an elective for her. It was a refuge. A place where expectations were clear, effort was rewarded, and her presence mattered.

This was one of the first moments in my teaching career when I truly grasped the social and emotional power of musicking—not as a theory, not as a research citation, but as lived reality.

Music didn't fix Ashley's life.
But it stabilized something essential.

Around this time, something else shifted—this time in me.

I realized I was no longer showing up to work motivated by obligation, evaluation, or even professional ambition. I was motivated by my students.

Ashley did not become a different person.
She became more fully herself.

Harvey: When Time Did the Teaching

Harvey entered my program in sixth grade—a year I have consistently found to be the most challenging in K–12 education. Sixth grade sits at the intersection of childhood and adolescence, where emotional regulation, identity, and impulse control are all in flux.

From the beginning, Harvey struggled.

He entered the band room with energy that had nowhere to go. He ran. He disrupted. Teaching him basic classroom etiquette—how to move safely, how to attend to others, how to respect shared space—became a daily task.

And when it came time to play his instrument, he struggled there too.

There were moments when I genuinely questioned whether I could help him. Meetings were held—with parents, guidance counselors, administrators. We discussed behavior plans. We even discussed whether band class was the right fit.

Still, I stayed consistent.

I taught the same way every day. I held boundaries. I showed up regulated. I allowed breaks when needed—not as avoidance, but as support. And I did not lower my belief in who Harvey could become, even when his behavior suggested otherwise.

Progress came slowly.
Almost imperceptibly.

Over the course of two years, something shifted. Harvey became more regulated. He learned how to focus. His playing improved steadily, until one day, it was simply solid.

By seventh grade, Harvey was performing just as well as his peers.
Focused.
Engaged.
Part of the culture.

This experience reshaped how I understand development.

Where a student begins tells us very little about where they can go—especially when we allow time, structure, and belief to do their work. Harvey did not need to be removed.

He needed to be held.

That realization changed my teaching in one of the most profound ways it ever has.

EPILOGUE

Becoming Without Arrival

If you have reached this point, you have walked a long road with me.

Not simply through events or milestones, but through formation—through moments where identity was shaped quietly, often without permission, and sometimes without clarity. This book has moved through childhood and classrooms, stages and studios, certainty and collapse. And now, here at the end, it feels important to name something plainly:

This is not the end of a journey.
It is a pause before return.

The pages stop here. The work does not.

What Changed Along the Way

I did not write this book to resolve my story. I wrote it to understand it.

What changed—slowly, almost imperceptibly—was not the difficulty of the work, but my relationship to it. I came to understand teaching not as a role I stepped into, but as an identity that had been forming long before I stood at the front of a classroom. I began to see that artistry was not something I had to abandon in order to teach well—it was something that sharpened my capacity to listen, to respond, and to care.

I also learned that struggle is not evidence of inadequacy. It is often evidence of engagement. Excellence, I discovered, is rarely clean. And care—real care—demands more than enthusiasm. It requires presence, humility, and endurance.

Nothing resolved neatly.
But much integrated.

And that, I've learned, is often the most honest form of growth.

Teaching as a Long Game

There is a quiet myth in education that one day we will arrive.

That at some point we will feel fully prepared, fully confident, fully certain of who we are as teachers. That the questions will slow. That the doubts will disappear. That the work will finally feel manageable.

I no longer believe that.

Teaching is not something we arrive at. It is something we practice. It is shaped through repetition, reflection, missteps, repair, and return. It evolves as we evolve. The pressure to be fully formed—to feel ready before beginning—is a burden no educator can actually carry.

If you are waiting to feel ready, you may be waiting forever.

What sustains us instead is willingness: to learn, to adapt, to remain curious, and to keep showing up—even when certainty is unavailable. That has been true at every stage of my life, from music to teaching to leadership. Becoming did not happen all at once.

It happened because I stayed.

Reclaiming Dignity in the Work

Teaching has a way of stripping things away if we let it.

Joy can erode under pressure.
Agency can shrink beneath systems.
Creativity can be flattened by compliance.
Humanity can become an afterthought when outcomes are prioritized over conditions.

And yet—this work still matters.

Teaching is not transactional labor. It is relational craft. It is moral work. It is the daily, often invisible act of standing with others as they try to become themselves. That work deserves dignity—not romanticization, not martyrdom, but respect.

There is nothing small about shaping environments where people feel seen, challenged, and capable of growth. There is nothing weak about caring deeply while holding high expectations. There is nothing naïve about believing that who we are matters just as much as what we teach.

To Those Who Are Struggling Right Now

If you are exhausted, doubting, or quietly wondering whether you can keep going, I want to speak to you directly.

Struggle does not disqualify you.
Difficulty does not mean you are failing.
Needing support does not make you weak.

Some seasons of teaching are about survival. Some are about rebuilding. Some are about questioning everything you thought you knew. I have lived all of them. Staying—when done with intention and honesty—can be one of the bravest acts there is.

And leaving, when done with clarity and care, can also be an act of integrity.

What matters is not endurance for its own sake, but alignment with purpose. You are allowed to name what you need. You are allowed to change. You are allowed to become again.

To Those Who Are Thriving

If teaching currently feels aligned—if your work feels life-giving and rooted—I honor that too.

Hold it with humility.
Protect it with care.
And remember that not everyone around you is standing where you are.

Your steadiness can become shelter for someone else. Your curiosity can keep complacency at bay. Your joy can remind the rest of us what is possible.

Thriving is not a finish line.

It is a responsibility.

Returning the Book to You

This book does not ask you to adopt my philosophy.

It asks something quieter.

What has your life already taught you about teaching?
What experiences are shaping you—even now?
What might you stop resisting, and begin listening to instead?

You do not need my answers.

You already have your own.

The work is not to become someone else.
It is to become more fully yourself—on purpose.

Final Offering

I believe this:

Teaching matters because people matter.
And people are always in the process of becoming.

That is not a problem to solve.
It is a truth to honor.

Becoming is the work.

Stay with it.

About The Author

Dr. Richard A. Fields, Ed.D. is an educator, musician, and scholar whose work centers on teacher formation, music education, and the lived experiences that shape professional identity. He currently serves as a Visiting Assistant Professor of Music and works across K–12 and higher education contexts, bringing a career that bridges performance, pedagogy, and educational leadership.

Dr. Fields began his professional life as a classical trumpet performer, studying and performing at the highest levels before navigating a series of personal, physical, and professional reinventions that ultimately led him into teaching. His work as a K–12 music educator in New York City public schools included building instrumental and vocal programs from the ground up, securing significant resources for students, and teaching across diverse educational settings. These experiences continue to inform his approach to curriculum design, teacher education, and mentorship.

He earned his Doctor of Education degree from Teachers College, Columbia University, where his research focused on identity, access, and persistence among musicians from historically underrepresented backgrounds. His scholarship and teaching are grounded in the belief that teaching is not merely a technical skill, but an identity shaped through lived experience, reflection, and care.

Dr. Fields continues to perform, teach, and write at the intersection of artistry, education, and human development.

www.ingramcontent.com/pod-product-compliance
Lightning Source LLC
Chambersburg PA
CBHW031043110426
42740CB00048B/979